The Vibrant Sage

Arousing Energy for Health and Happiness

Nancy Waring, MS

No part of this publication may be reproduced, stored in a retrieval system, or transmitted in any form or by any means—electronic, photocopying, recording, or otherwise—without prior written permission, except in the case of brief excerpts in critical reviews and articles. For permission requests, contact the author at nancy@thevibrantsage.com.

All rights reserved.

Copyright © 2024 Nancy Waring

ISBN: 9798334040311

The author disclaims responsibility for adverse effects or consequences from the misapplication or injudicious use of the information contained in this book. Mention of resources and associations does not imply an endorsement.

DEDICATION

This book is dedicated to my father, Henry Thomas Waring. Dad, your unwavering courage and relentless determination to embrace life with passion, even in the face of seemingly insurmountable challenges, have left an indelible mark on my heart. Against all odds, you defied expectations and lived more than thirty years beyond what was thought possible, a testament to your resilience and strength of spirit.

I cherish the memories of our time together, and I hold dear the lessons you imparted to me. Your guidance and wisdom have empowered me to confront my own obstacles, pursue my passions, and strive to live each day to its fullest. It is through your example that I have come to understand the true essence of being a Vibrant Sage—a journey of vitality, purpose, and unwavering resilience.

Though you may no longer be with us, your legacy lives on in the lives you touched and the lessons you taught. I love you dearly, Dad, and I am forever grateful for the gift of your presence in my life.

CONTENTS

PREFACE 1
INTRODUCTION 7
PART ONE: Listening from the Inside 11
   1. A RUDE AWAKENING: CHASING FITNESS 13
   2. UNRAVELING WELLNESS: A GENETIC ODYSSEY 21
   3. YOUR BODY COMMUNICATES –
      LISTEN AND LEARN 33

PART TWO: Foundation for Arousing Health &
              Happiness—The Five Pillars 45
   4. PILLAR ONE: BREATH
      EMBRACING YOUR BREATH,
      YOUR POWER SOURCE 47
   5. PILLAR TWO: MOVEMENT
      EMBRACING MOVEMENT, NO GYM REQUIRED 79
   6. PILLAR THREE: NUTRITION
      EVOLOVING NUTRITION . . .
      IT'S NOT ABOUT THE CALORIES 119
   7. PILLAR FOUR: SLEEP
      QUALITY SLEEP: TIME TO RECHARGE
      YOUR CELLS 149
   8. PILLAR FIVE: PURPOSE
      PURPOSE-DRIVEN HEALTH:
      THE SECRET TO A VIBRANT LIFE 185

PART THREE: Sagehood 213
   9. BECOMING A VIBRANT SAGE 215
   10. PASSION AND INTIMACY: THE POWER OF
       CONNECTION AND SEXUALITY......................223
   11. YOUR FUTURE IS NOW 247

ACKNOWLEDGMENTS..253
RESOURCES 257
CONNECT WITH THE EXPERTS..261
ABOUT THE AUTHOR 263

PREFACE

Dear Reader,

The book you hold in your hands is a true labor of love; it has taken over three years and three complete revisions to become what you now have before you. When I started writing this book, I was unsure of its direction, beyond the broad scope of wanting to offer insights for improving health and fitness. However, as time passed, I was drawn deeper into the exploration of what it truly means to thrive, particularly as we navigate the complexities of aging.

Over the years, my journey has been one of personal and professional growth, and I've expanded my understanding of health and vitality in ways I never anticipated. I came to realize that true wellness begins from within, rooted in every cell of our being. Yet too often, we look outward for answers, overlooking the profound wisdom and potential that resides within each of us.

My quest to understand the essence of health and vitality, and how it unfolds across the various stages of life, began over a decade ago. It was fueled by a burning desire to uncover the secrets of holistic well-being and to share these insights with others. Little did I know that this pursuit would lead me to the profound concept of becoming a vibrant sage—a journey of self-discovery and empowerment that transcends mere physical health.

In February 2010, within the walls of an inpatient rehabilitation center, I encountered a man I will refer to as Lou. Despite his silent demeanor, Lou's presence left an indelible mark on me. He was a living testament to the consequences of neglecting one's well-being.

Lou's struggle stemmed from a massive stroke, which left him unable to speak, swallow, or comprehend basic instructions. As I visited him daily, I pondered the chain of events that had led to his condition. It became clear that Lou's stroke and subsequent challenges were not sudden occurrences, but rather the culmination of years, perhaps decades, of unhealthy habits.

His story served as a sobering reminder of the interconnectedness between our daily choices and long-term health outcomes. In Lou's silent resilience, I found inspiration to deepen my commitment to promoting holistic well-being.

Even though I only knew him briefly, Lou's story continues to resonate with me, urging me to embrace each day with gratitude and to advocate for a lifestyle that nurtures both body and soul.

After nearly three decades as a speech language pathologist and interacting with thousands of individuals, that day marked a profound turning point in my life. Witnessing Lou's struggle stirred a deep sense of sadness within me, knowing that his condition probably could have been prevented. It was then that I made a solemn commitment—to dedicate myself to helping others lead healthy, fulfilling lives and to prevent the onset of chronic lifestyle disorders. This experience ignited a passionate pursuit to become a proactive advocate for holistic well-being, supporting adults in creating sustainable lifestyles, whether they're in the workforce or enjoying retirement. Each day since has been a reminder of life's preciousness, with its myriad of challenges and joys, guiding me on a journey of purpose and resilience.

Parents are often our greatest teachers, shaping our understanding of life and health. My father embodied the essence of vitality and purpose. At ninety-eight, he defied the odds, living each day with a vigor that belied his age. His commitment to health was unwavering—he understood that maintaining vitality required more than mere existence; it demanded purposeful living. Through diligent self-care practices and a deep sense of well-being, he cultivated resilience in the face of adversity. Despite facing prostate cancer in his seventies and the loss of vision in his nineties, he continued to prioritize his well-being through wholesome nutrition, regular exercise, and a deep connection with loved ones.

Conversely, my mother's journey was marked by struggles with chronic illness and mental health issues, and she succumbed to the ravages of chronic obstructive pulmonary disease (COPD) and depression at the young age of sixty-two. Her story serves as a poignant reminder of the profound impact that lifestyle choices and mental well-being have on health outcomes. Despite her battle with illness, she lacked the sense of purpose and resilience that characterized my father's approach to life.

In a moment of reflection and meditation, my mother's spirit reached out to me, guiding me through the process of writing this book. Her silent encouragement served as a reminder of the importance of her story and the message it carries. Through her struggles and untimely passing, she imparted invaluable lessons about the fragility of life and the necessity of prioritizing mental well-being alongside physical health.

Reflecting on their divergent paths, I've come to appreciate the transformative power of healthy behaviors, self-care, and purpose-driven living. While my father's proactive approach to health enabled him to thrive well into his nineties, my mother's struggles underscore the importance of addressing both physical and mental well-being. Their experiences have profoundly shaped my journey, reinforcing this book's central theme: the significance of healthy lifestyle choices, self-care practices, and finding purpose in every aspect of life.

In honoring my parents' legacies, I hope to inspire you to embrace a holistic approach to health, one that prioritizes both physical vitality and a sense of purpose in living.

As we begin this journey of self-discovery and vitality, it's essential to understand the landscape of health and well-being. Chronic diseases, defined as conditions lasting more than one year and often requiring ongoing management, comprise a range of physical and mental health conditions, significantly impact our quality of life and longevity. They encompass ailments such as heart disease, diabetes, cancer, hypertension, stroke, obesity, and respiratory disorders.

According to the Centers for Disease Control and Prevention (CDC), nearly 60 percent of adults grapple with at least one chronic condition, underscoring the urgent need for proactive approaches to health and wellness.[1]

Understanding the impact of chronic diseases is not merely an exercise in statistics; it's a reflection of the complex interplay between lifestyle choices, genetic predispositions, and environmental factors. As you read this book, filled with narratives of resilience, purpose, and vitality, let each story serve as a testament to the transformative power of adopting a holistic approach to health.

Whether you've personally faced chronic illness challenges or seek to prevent their onset, know that you are not alone on this journey. Together, let us navigate the terrain of well-being, guided

---

[1] Timothy Jay Carney and Jennifer L. Wiltz, "Advancing Chronic Disease Practice Through the CDC Data Modernization Initiative," Centers for Disease Control and Prevention (CDC), November 30, 2023, accessed April 11, 2023, https://www.cdc.gov/pcd/issues/2023/23_0120.htm#:~:text=Chronic%20disease%20affects%206%20in,health%20care%20spending%20(1).

PREFACE

by the wisdom of those who have walked before us and the promise of a future filled with joy, happiness, and vibrant health.

Within these pages, you'll find insights, wisdom, and practical strategies to empower you along the way. From simple daily habits to profound shifts in mindset, each step will bring you closer to embodying the vibrant sage within.

While on my own journey of self-discovery, I realized that true vitality transcends the physical realm—it emanates from the depths of our being, igniting our passions and fueling our dreams. Through setbacks and triumphs alike, I've learned that the key to unlocking our full potential lies in welcoming every aspect of our journey with unwavering enthusiasm and resilience.

The book is a testament to this journey—a culmination of years of research, introspection, and growth. It's a mirror reflecting my evolution and a guide illuminating your path to self-discovery. Whether you're reading as a vibrant sage yourself or sharing this gift with loved ones, know that each page is infused with heartfelt gratitude and profound wisdom.

So, as you begin this adventure, remember to embrace the present moment and trust in the power within you. For it's through embracing your inner sage that you'll unlock the secrets to a life filled with joy, vitality, and fulfillment. The time is now—let your inner light shine brightly for all the world to see.

With gratitude and anticipation,
Nancy

INTRODUCTION

Birth is a start and death is its end and between birth and death is a journey of life; travel with peace and love before it ends.
— Ehsan Sehgal

Welcome to the Journey Ahead

Life is marked by light and shadow, triumphs, and tribulations. As I reflect on my unique path, I'm reminded of another favorite Ehsan Sehgal quote: "Life is a journey, with problems to solve, lessons to learn, but most of all, experiences to enjoy."

My journey began amidst the serene landscapes of Southern Maryland—a place where community thrived and nature beckoned exploration. Growing up as a natural tomboy, I spent my days immersed in adventures, exploring the woods, climbing trees, and riding my bike.

Transitioning into adulthood brought new challenges and opportunities. Leaving behind the tranquility of farm life, I moved to the bustling metropolis of Boston for college, where I discovered a newfound love for movement and physical activity. Amidst the rigors of academia, I found solace in swimming, cycling, and running—activities that would become integral to my self-discovery and renewal.

In 2008, I received a random postcard promoting the opportunity to participate in a marathon with Team in Training that reignited a spark within me. At forty-seven, I dared to challenge my perceived limitations and embarked on a transformative journey of renewal and reinvention. The marathon became a metaphor for my life—a journey filled with obstacles, challenges, and moments of profound growth.

As I crossed the finish line, tears of joy and relief streamed down my cheeks. That moment ignited a fire within me and sparked the profound epiphany that if I had unwavering determination, I could achieve anything. For the first time, I glimpsed the athlete within me, rekindling a belief that anything is possible, regardless of age.

Deciding to transition from speech pathology to fitness coaching, my new mission emerged: to empower others to prioritize their health and vitality. Through certifications, coaching, and writing, I inspire individuals to embrace a lifestyle of energy, wisdom, and vitality.

Now, as the author of *The Vibrant Sage*, I share my journey and philosophy of thriving at every stage of life with the hope that my message resonates with readers seeking to embrace their own journey toward vibrancy and fulfillment.

This book is divided into three sections:

In Part One, I'll guide you through my personal odyssey, where you'll witness moments of triumph and growth. These stories serve as a foundation for the transformative ideas shared in each of the five pillars of vibrant living.

Part Two explores the heart of our journey, delving into breath, movement, nutrition, sleep, and purpose. Through scientific insights and personal anecdotes, you'll uncover practical strategies to enhance vitality and well-being.

INTRODUCTION

In Part Three, you'll find thought-provoking reflections, an illuminating interview, and captivating scenarios that will inspire you to embrace vitality with authenticity and purpose.

As we navigate this exploration of vibrant aging, I invite you to reflect on your unique path and chart your course toward a life filled with vitality, joy, and purpose.

Guided by the wisdom of your past and the promise of your future, let's embrace the symphony of life, knowing that every experience contributes to the beautiful tapestry of your existence.

PART ONE

Listening from the Inside

CHAPTER 1

A RUDE AWAKENING: CHASING FITNESS

Knowing yourself is the beginning of all wisdom.
— Aristotle

For the first half-century of my life, I was anything but a sage. While I had amassed a wealth of knowledge, wisdom often eluded me, and common sense occasionally felt in short supply. My lifestyle habits, once mere pursuits, transformed into obsessive health and fitness routines that did not yield the expected benefits. At the cellular level, my body was aging at an accelerated pace, which took me years to acknowledge.

It is from my journey to rejuvenate my fitness and well-being after crossing the half-century mark that I offer my experiences and profound insights. Without the trials, tribulations, and triumphs, I wouldn't have the wisdom I now hold or the insight to grasp the profound truth that life is a remarkable, challenging, and ceaseless voyage of self-discovery.

Fit on the Outside . . . Unwell on the Inside

Exercise had always been a part of my adult life, a mix of activities like swimming, skiing, cycling, group fitness classes, and even the hustle and bustle of raising three kids. It was a jigsaw puzzle of joyful moments, but it was rarely structured, regimented, or goal driven.

That all changed in early 2008. One crisp January day, an ordinary postcard from the Leukemia & Lymphoma Society's Team in Training program arrived in my mailbox. It touted an opportunity to run for a cause, offering two daunting choices: a half marathon or a full one, in the beautiful city of San Diego. Sixteen weeks of rigorous training awaited those brave enough to take the plunge. I admit, until that moment, I had no clue what the distance of a full marathon was—26.2 miles, to be exact.

For some reason, I was intrigued. So the first step on this unexpected journey was to learn more. A few weeks after receiving the postcard, I went to an informational session. As soon as I entered the room, I felt the atmosphere crackle with infectious energy. And the enthusiasm was palpable when those who had walked this path before us shared their stories.

One after another, speakers stood up to share their remarkable journeys. Some recounted their marathon triumphs, while others expressed gratitude for the hope and support that fighting cancer had brought them. They called us heroes, and in that moment, it was impossible to resist their call.

As I reflect on that pivotal postcard's arrival, I'm still at a loss for a concrete reason why I did not dismiss it like countless other postcards and flyers. It was as if an inner voice guided my hand, compelling me to attend the meeting.

That cryptic intuition became the catalyst for a remarkable journey, forever altering a part of my life. Little did I know that this ordinary postcard would steer me toward an extraordinary adventure and the start of a passionate obsession.

It started innocently. We were given a training schedule, and every Saturday, we met as a team to train for the event. Some of the runners were seasoned and had run many marathons, but for many of us, it was our first time. Our coaches held our hands and gave each of us the support and encouragement we needed so we wouldn't give up. It was grueling at times but not insurmountable. This experience was nothing short of extraordinary.

Almost six months after receiving the fortuitous postcard, on Sunday, June 1, 2008, I ran my first marathon. As I crossed the finish line, my eyes welled with tears. It wasn't just the pain in my legs that brought me to tears; it was the profound realization that I could accomplish anything I set my mind to. The sense of empowerment was overwhelming. It may have been the first time in my life I achieved a goal that, less than a year before, seemed impossible.

My transformation from a sporadic fitness enthusiast to an unrelenting runner, obsessed with the pursuit of strength and speed, unfolded gradually. In the first couple of years, I enjoyed a mix of fitness activities, including running, without any specific goals in mind. But something remarkable began to stir within me.

In the first year after that marathon, I participated in no less than eight races. The thrill of the track, the pulse of the competition, and the joy of self-improvement fueled my newfound passion. I was not only running; I was racing, and I was getting faster with every stride. The competitive drive that lay dormant within me suddenly roared to life.

Running was no longer just a means of general fitness; it had evolved into an unquenchable obsession to reach new heights of speed and performance. I was conquering races of various lengths—three-, six-, ten-, and thirteen-mile races. The pursuit of excellence became my daily mantra.

For a time, I managed to maintain a delicate balance between my commitments to work, family, and my ever-growing fitness obsession. And in 2012, something profound shifted. My body underwent a remarkable transformation, sculpting itself into its leanest, strongest form. I shed at least ten pounds, my muscles became chiseled, my abdominal muscles had definition—a three pack—and my running speeds reached unprecedented levels. Suddenly, I felt like an athlete, a sensation previously foreign to me. It was an intoxicating and invigorating experience.

What struck me most was that this transformation occurred after I had crossed the fifty-year mark. It was a testament to the power of relentless dedication and unwavering passion. It was just exercise, or so I thought. Little did I know that my energy and vibrancy were reaching their zenith.

The Boston Marathon holds a unique distinction among races; it is one of the few events that requires participants to qualify. At my age, the qualifying time stood at under four hours. With this goal in mind, I kicked off a year of relentless training.

My singular focus was clear: to qualify for the prestigious Boston Marathon in 2013 so that I could run the iconic race the following year. But to qualify, I had to shave at least seventy minutes from my first marathon's time—a monumental challenge. My commitment knew no bounds, and I trained with unwavering passion and purpose.

In my relentless pursuit of this ambitious goal, I made a crucial decision—I hired a running coach to provide support, encouragement, and expert guidance. During my training sessions, I felt an unwavering sense of invincibility, fueled by an incredible surge of energy and resilience.

By the time of the qualifying race, I felt ready—strong, confident, and even gleeful. The qualifying event was the Long Island

Marathon. It was a beautiful early May morning; the air crisp, the temperature a perfect fifty degrees. The race felt effortless, a stark contrast to my first marathon five years earlier. As I crossed the finish line in just three hours and fifty-three minutes, I still felt energized, as if I could run another one. No cramping or tears, just pure joy! I had done it—I had achieved a goal that just a few years earlier, I would never have dared to dream. Yet, this dream had indeed come true. I had successfully secured my qualification for the Boston Marathon—a testament to my relentless dedication. Little did I realize, however, the profound toll this arduous journey was taking on my physical well-being.

Shortly after securing my qualification, I noticed something I hadn't experienced before—more frequent and intense cramping in my calves and hamstrings. Yet I chose to dismiss these warning signs, convinced that pushing through the discomfort was the only path to progress. After all, "no pain, no gain," right?

For the next few months, I pushed harder, ignoring the cramps that could strike at any moment. However, there were even more insidious symptoms that I chose to ignore. I felt constantly fatigued. My ability to concentrate dwindled, and I found myself making careless mistakes at work. Occasionally, I struggled to retain information.

Was this the price I had to pay for pushing myself to the limit? But at the time, I remained oblivious, even though friends and loved ones began to express their concerns. They would ask, "Nancy, are you all right?"

From the outside, I still appeared fit and strong. However, inside my body, at the cellular level, something sinister was brewing. Inflammation was silently ravaging my body and mind, setting the stage for a challenge that would test my resilience and determination.

Wisdom Eluded Me

My body had been desperately trying to communicate with me, sending signals that grew louder and louder, yet I stubbornly refused to listen. I held on to the belief that I was strong, unbreakable, and unstoppable. But the turning point arrived in the fall.

As the sun painted the pristine October morning with its warm rays, the temperature was perfect—not too hot, not too cold. The excitement of my first major race since earning my spot in the Boston Marathon pulsed through my veins. It was the Entenmann's Great South Bay Half Marathon, a challenging 13.1 miles.

I felt strong as I stood at the starting line, but around mile three, without warning, my left hamstring seized up in a painful cramp. Yet I was undeterred. This sensation was not entirely foreign to me; only once before had it been so severe that it forced me to halt my run. On this fateful day, around mile six, the relentless cramping finally subsided, and I felt invigorated once more.

Crossing the finish line, a triumphant realization washed over me—I had achieved a personal best, completing the race in an astonishing one hour and fifty-one minutes. The feeling was nothing short of exhilarating. Once again, I had pushed my limits and broken my own records.

The post-race celebration was a blast. After enjoying some food and a beer, I headed back to my car, which was about a half mile away. As I began to jog toward my car, my left hamstring suddenly cramped with such intensity that my left leg became immobile. My right leg moved forward, and I fell—a hard, painful fall. Blood streamed from my right knee and hand, and the screen of my phone lay shattered. I mustered the strength to get back on my feet, slowly hobbling to my car, all the while nursing physical pain and the sting of humiliation.

In that moment, my previously solid facade of fitness crumbled—a stark reminder that even the best intentions can lead to unforeseen outcomes. My body had been trying to communicate with me, but my ego held sway, until my body reached its breaking point.

As I picked myself up from that fall, I could not help but wonder: How often do we push ourselves beyond our limits, blinded by our ambitions? How well do we truly know ourselves, both physically and mentally? These questions would become the compass guiding me on a new phase of my journey as I ventured into the uncharted territory of listening to my body and understanding the intricate connection between physical strength and inner wisdom.

The New York City Marathon loomed just three weeks away, an event I could not have imagined participating in a few years earlier. I was driven to still compete, so I sought rest and professional help, including a sports chiropractor, massage therapist, and myofascial release therapist. However, none of these treatments provided relief.

Eventually, an orthopedist took an X-ray that revealed a torn labrum in my left hip. The hip labrum is a resilient cartilage that provides both support and flexibility to the hip joint. This discovery explained the excruciating pain that surged whenever I tried to walk briskly, let alone run. There was no way I could race.

The Emergence of the Vibrant Sage

Despite the image of fitness I saw when I looked in the mirror, the reality was that I was not genuinely healthy from the inside, at the cellular level. Now I began to question not only how all of this had happened but, more critically, what it truly means to be healthy.

Little did I know that this simple question would lead me on a remarkable journey that made running my first marathon easy in comparison. Never had I even considered that you can look fit on the outside, while on the inside, your body can be fighting to keep you strong and healthy. The events that unfolded afterward prompted me to explore the fascinating world of epigenetics and DNA, fields that shed light on the long-term impact of our lifestyle choices on our cellular health.

These experiences led me to a deeper revelation—the discovery of the five pillars of vibrant aging. These pillars would become the cornerstone of my path to becoming a vibrant sage.

You may be wondering, what is a vibrant sage? My definition of a vibrant sage is an individual who defies age stereotypes and embraces a journey of lifelong learning and growth. They prioritize their health and well-being and embody a zest for life that knows no limits.

Each of us is on an ongoing journey of self-discovery. I invite you now to reflect on your life. How well do you truly know yourself, and what is the relationship between your physical strength and inner wisdom? What aspirations, ambitions, or dreams have you chased without fully understanding their impact on your well-being? Consider these questions as we delve deeper into the world of epigenetics and explore the five pillars of vibrant aging. In the chapters ahead, you will discover how these pillars can transform your life, just as they have transformed mine. Your path to becoming a vibrant sage awaits.

Are you ready to embark on this transformative journey?

CHAPTER 2

UNRAVELING WELLNESS: A GENETIC ODYSSEY

Genes are like the story, and DNA is the language that the story is written in.
— Sam Kean

For years, I whimsically attributed various aspects of my identity to the enigmatic orchestration of my genes. My deoxyribonucleic acid (DNA) served as the conductor, orchestrating the harmonious notes of my introverted tendencies, my relentless urge to help others, my wanderlust for exploring new horizons, and my insatiable thirst for knowledge. It was a combination of my innate curiosity for exploring new horizons and my quest for knowledge that led me, a country girl from Southern Maryland, to Boston University in 1978. It was here in the bustling rhythm of city life that I thrived for six exhilarating years, eagerly seizing every chance to connect with individuals from all corners of the globe as I navigated the exciting transition into adulthood, all while pursuing and completing both my undergraduate and graduate degrees in speech pathology. They say that when you pursue your passion, work transforms into a labor of love. I can confidently attest that during my three-decade career as a speech pathologist, I rarely experienced the sensation of "work." Consequently, I had never contemplated "retirement" or any other career.

Becoming a personal trainer and health coach began innocently enough, driven by my quest to uncover the most effective methods to optimize my health, particularly as I aspired to excel in running. After taking a weekend course in February 2012, I had my first fitness certification and donned the mantle of a personal trainer. With this new knowledge, I followed routines and programs with the goal of perfecting my running prowess. Steadily, I got faster, stronger, and leaner, but never feeling satisfied, I kept pushing myself harder and harder. However, following that fateful fall, I stood at a crossroads, my belief in fitness forever altered. After a few months of soul-searching, I realized that genuine health and fitness were not confined to mere appearances, physical prowess, or generic fitness programs.

Change was inevitable. I could not run. Now what? Instead of fitness programs geared toward running, I began to research and explore various methods of cardiovascular and strength training. Equipped with knowledge, motivation, and the desire to listen to my body, I started on a journey of self-exploration in the pursuit of perfecting my fitness and health.

I went looking for alternative ways to maintain my lean body and cardio fitness level that did not hurt my body. Cardio machines were so boring. Thankfully, I found two heart-pumping activities that I enjoyed: cycling and swimming. I even added a new certification to my accomplishments—I became an indoor spin instructor, not only to maintain my cardiovascular fitness and strength but also to guide others on their paths to wellness.

Next, strength training. Previously, my strength training focused on heavy weights, meaning more weight and fewer repetitions. Now I switched to not just lighter weights but resistance bands and TRX suspension training, and yes, another certification as a level-one TRX trainer. I also added a weekly Les Miles body pump class, which helped me stay strong.

Next change, diet. While I ate whole foods, I transitioned to the Paleo way of eating, meaning I tried to eat the way our ancestors did thousands of years ago. Meat, vegetables, fruits, and nuts/seeds were the staples of my diet. Processed foods, which included but were not limited to breads, sugar, and dairy, were eliminated. I lost a few pounds and felt much better overall, but I did struggle with living this lifestyle after six months or so. Even to this day, my diet reflects more of this way of eating—whole foods, but not too strict. Over the next three years, from 2013 to early 2016, a gradual transformation unfolded. My energy levels soared, and my mood lifted significantly. Gone were the days when concerned friends inquired about my well-being; instead, they marveled at the new vibrancy in my life. I had not only maintained a solid cardiovascular fitness level, but I had also significantly enhanced my body's strength and resilience. While I may not have been winning medals or chasing after an ideal skinny physique, I was achieving something far more precious: the gradual restoration of my health, vitality, and a renewed zest for life.

Combining my personal journey, which began when I decided to improve my health after turning fifty, with my newfound knowledge related to health and fitness, I began to wonder about many of my speech clients. Especially those who had suffered a stroke, dementia, or had developed an autoimmune disorder—could changes in lifestyle have prevented the communication disorder or helped reduce the symptoms or severity of the disability? This internal switch is what triggered me to transition from a speech pathologist to a fitness and health coach.

It was during this gradual transformation that an epiphany struck me like a bolt of lightning. I realized that my true purpose was to empower adults to not only safeguard themselves against chronic lifestyle disorders but to enjoy life with vibrant health. While my journey had taken me from speech pathologist to fitness and health coach, it was my unwavering dedication to improving lives that remained a constant thread, weaving the tapestry of my professional identity.

Unlocking the Genetic Clues to Your Unique Potential

As we uncover the power of our genetic clues, it is crucial to understand what DNA is. Simply put, DNA, or deoxyribonucleic acid, is the molecule that carries genetic information for an organism's development and functioning. It is composed of two linked strands forming a double helix that resembles a twisted ladder.

While I had a basic understanding of DNA's role in diagnosing genetic conditions and assessing disease risk, my perspective broadened when I embarked on a transformative journey that revealed the evolving focus of genetics, where we find mutations and variants in our DNA to improve fitness and health. It brought back vivid memories of a conference I attended two decades ago, where the groundbreaking Human Genome Project (HGP) was discussed with awe and anticipation.

At the conference at Columbia University, which was focused on Velocardiofacial syndrome, now known as DiGeorge syndrome, Dr. Robert Shprintzen took the stage. His visionary words were that this project would one day help scientists and doctors prevent and cure diseases and genetic disorders, such as DiGeorge syndrome. The image that he presented of a world where everyone was healthy and free of dis-ease sparked a curiosity within me that lay dormant for years, waiting to be awakened. In 2003, the culmination of the Human Genome Project marked a turning point in science. At that time, it was widely believed that our destiny was locked within the codes of our DNA. However, as time passed, science revealed a different truth.

Reflecting on this odyssey from the early 1990s to the present day, I marvel at our collective evolution in deciphering the language of our genes. Each discovery along the way has brought us closer to unraveling the mysteries of our health and potential. The seeds of curiosity sown all those years ago have grown into a profound sense of wonder, inspiring my transformative quest to unlock the hidden secrets within my DNA.

An Ounce of Prevention

As I shared in Chapter One, wisdom had often eluded me, especially concerning my body's needs. Chronic pain and fatigue had become my constant companions. I knew what I needed to do—slow down and stop pushing my body so hard. Yet my ego won; my appearance and performance motivated me to keep moving forward. I simply did not know there was any other way.

In October 2017, I found myself amidst the buzz of the Employer Healthcare and Benefits Conference in Los Angeles. With over two thousand attendees and a lineup of speakers and vendors at the forefront of the health and wellness space, it was an international event bursting with knowledge and innovation.

As I meticulously prepared for the conference, scouting for professionals to connect with, two vendors stood out like beacons: DNAFit Life Sciences, Ltd. and Silverberry Genomix. Their tantalizing promise to unlock the untapped potential of our DNA for optimal health and wellness captivated me from the start. Both offered a distinct set of insights and solutions that piqued my curiosity and ignited a fervor to dive headfirst into the fascinating world of genetic wellness. Driven by my eagerness to explore this intriguing realm of genetic insight and uncover its potential applications for enhanced health and well-being, I swiftly arranged meetings with both companies.

Questions swirled in my mind: What is a DNA assessment? Could understanding my DNA have spared me from that life-altering fall? What revelations could a DNA assessment bring? How might this knowledge transform lives? Could it be the key to better health and vitality? My intellectual curiosity was in overdrive.

As I engaged in enlightening discussions with Noah Voreades from DNAFit Life Sciences, Ltd., and delved into conversations with Shayan R. Mashatian, the visionary CEO of Silverberry Genomix, I was struck by the incredible strides that were being made in scientific understanding. It wasn't just a personal curiosity; it was a professional calling. The profound potential to use this new scientific knowledge to better my clients' lives ignited a passionate drive within me. I felt compelled to seek answers about my own DNA so that I could help guide my clients toward personalized fitness and health lifestyles that were aligned with their unique genetic profiles.

In my pursuit of comprehensive understanding, I decided to take both DNA tests. The process was surprisingly straightforward, involving a simple saliva swab sample dispatched to a laboratory for analysis. Yet the anticipation that gripped me during the three to four weeks of waiting was akin to a fervent quest for answers.

This quest was driven by a dual motivation. On one hand, I yearned to unlock the secrets of the best dietary and fitness strategies, tailored precisely to my unique genetic profile. On the other hand, I wanted answers to the persistent mysteries surrounding my frequent aches, pains, and cramping—a desire to delve into the depths of my DNA to uncover the root causes.

But this journey went even deeper. It aimed to illuminate the factors that might have played a role in the fateful fall I experienced a few years prior. These test results were about to reveal the secrets hidden within my DNA, offering a path to a more vibrant, healthy, and harmonious life.

Finally, the day arrived when the results appeared in my inbox. These were not just scientific facts; they were genetic insights about fitness and nutrition, akin to a roadmap to understanding myself better. Looking back, I couldn't help but wonder how having these DNA insights earlier might have altered my path.

The big question I had . . . Could the fall that led to my injury have been prevented?

I believe the answer is YES!

Here are a few of the significant and life-changing takeaways from my DNA assessment:

Fitness Insights

Power Versus Endurance Exercise to Optimize My Health

Our DNA influences are natural tendencies toward optimizing fitness, with more short, intense bursts of power—think heavy weights with fewer repetitions and shorter bursts of cardiovascular exercises (sprinting) versus lighter weights with more repetitions and cardio movements over a longer period of time (distant running). My DNA revealed that my body's genetic makeup leans toward endurance. On the DNA Fit test, I scored 38.5 for power and 61.5 for endurance, revealing a natural inclination toward endurance activities like distance running, cycling, and swimming for long periods of time. This further supports why I have never been a sprinter or quick at the beginning of any athletic task.

Body's Use of Oxygen

VO2 max relates to how efficiently the body uses oxygen for sustained high-intensity exercise. My high VO2 max means my body can efficiently use oxygen for sustained high-intensity exercise. This can be developed over time. But this further supports my strong engagement in moderate, steady activities, such as running long distances and cycling.

Recovery Time After Intense Exercise

Recovery time relates to how much time the body needs to truly recover from intensive exercise. While some people have very quick recovery time needs, my results revealed my body needs at least forty-eight hours of recovery between intense exercise. Unfortunately, I rarely took time for recovery. Sure, I knew that research suggested taking forty-eight hours, but I thought I had to keep pushing myself to get stronger. I had no idea I would have gotten stronger if I had taken time off from pushing myself.

Risk of Injury to Tendons and Ligaments

Injuries happen to everyone at some point. Yet our risk of sustaining an injury is significantly influenced by our DNA. My genes revealed a higher risk of injury, which aligned with my history of pushing through pain. For decades, I have tended to "roll/sprain" my right ankle. Knowing that I am at risk could have changed my mindset, and I would have listened to the various pains in my body.

Nutritional Insights

Optimal Diet

There is no optimal diet for everyone. A Mediterranean diet was recommended for optimizing my health. This is a very balanced diet that focuses on healthy fats, nuts and seeds, lean proteins, whole grains, and vegetables and fruits while limiting sugar and dairy.

Antioxidant Needs

Antioxidants are those vitamins that help your body recover from stress and hard work. More specifically, inflammation. My body requires more antioxidants to combat oxidative stress from exercise. My DNA suggests that my body does not perfect the absorption of these antioxidants, so it needs more—whether from supplements or food. Some of the most familiar antioxidants include vitamin C, vitamin E, and vitamin A.

Cruciferous Vegetable Needs

Cruciferous vegetables include vegetables such as cabbage, broccoli, and arugula. These types of vegetables have a mechanism that helps turn on specific genes to enhance the absorption of micronutrients—vitamins and minerals. They have anti-inflammatory and antioxidant properties. Results from my DNA assessments revealed that my body does not optimize absorption of these vegetables. Hence, my inherent need to increase my intake of these veggies was recommended for cellular and cardiovascular health.

Understanding my DNA has been a truly transformative journey that has illuminated my path to better health and fitness. As I dug deeper into the intricacies of my genetic makeup, I uncovered a profound connection between my genes and my overall well-being. This knowledge not only highlighted the importance of prioritizing recovery or fine-tuning my dietary choices, but it also sparked a fire within me to maximize my potential and defy the limitations that once held me back.

Looking back at my running journey, I now see the missed opportunities for growth and self-improvement. While I always ate a healthy diet, I didn't recognize that my body needed specific nutrients to flourish, to remain resilient, and to minimize discomfort. It's not just about avoiding junk food; it's about nourishing your body with the precise ingredients it craves for peak performance and vitality.

With the knowledge gleaned from my DNA insights, I have come to understand that incorporating regular recovery days, embracing an anti-inflammatory diet, and, most importantly, listening to my body's whispers during minor injuries could have altered the course of my journey. If only I had embraced these changes sooner, I genuinely believe I could have avoided that fateful fall, and today, I would still be relishing the exhilaration of running—a testament to the incredible power of knowledge, perseverance, and the unyielding spirit to overcome any challenge that comes our way.

The Symphony of Epigenetics and Lifestyle

I invite you to join me on an exploration of the interplay between our genes and the lifestyle choices we make. It's a journey that involves the symphony of epigenetics and lifestyle, where the music of your health plays its most profound notes.

Imagine your DNA is like the conductor of a grand orchestra, directing the performance of your body's genes. This is where the magic happens—the melody is not set in stone. It can change and adapt, just as a skilled conductor shapes the music.

This phenomenon is known as epigenetics, where our lifestyle choices and experiences can change how our genes are expressed. It's like having the power to rewrite parts of your genetic score. But how do we find the right tune, the harmonious melody that resonates with our unique genetic composition?

The key to unlocking your best health lies in something we often overlook—listening to your own body. This invaluable skill became clear to me back in 2013 when I recognized the need for change. It all started with tuning in to the signals my body was sending me.

Little did I know that listening to these signals would lead me to align my lifestyle with the unique composition of my DNA. While I experienced overall improvements in my health, it was not until I received my DNA results that I truly grasped the intricate interplay within our bodies—the symphony of wellness optimization.

Understanding my DNA was merely the prelude; the real transformation occurred when I began to heed the subtle cues my body was offering—those gentle whispers of fatigue, the beckoning of hunger, the rhythms of rest and recovery. These were the notes that, when heeded, composed the harmonious melody of well-being.

I invite you to become an active conductor in your own symphony of health. Beyond the physical sensations, remember to attune your senses to your emotions as well. Stress, happiness, sadness—each note contributes to the complex composition of your epigenetic melody, influencing how your genes harmonize with your overall well-being.

As we move forward, know that while a DNA assessment is a valuable tool, it is not a mandate. With age and wisdom, we become adept at deciphering our own unique genetic symphony, using our life experiences as guiding notes to orchestrate vibrant well-being. I, for one, did not have this wisdom from the outset, but I have embraced the path of discovery.

In the upcoming chapters, we'll venture deeper into the field of epigenetics, unveiling the mysteries behind lifestyle choices and empowering you with the knowledge to navigate your journey to health. It's a voyage where the wisdom of science harmonizes with the wisdom of life—a masterpiece in the making!

Are you ready to discover the vibrant sage within you?

CHAPTER 3

YOUR BODY COMMUNICATES – LISTEN AND LEARN

Your body is your best guide. It constantly tells you, in the form of pain or sensations, what is working for you and what is not.
—Hina Hashmi

An electrifying dance exists between our genes and our choices—a mesmerizing symphony that orchestrates how our genes respond to the harmonious or discordant melodies played by our environment and lifestyle choices and defies the notion that our destiny is etched in our DNA. Regardless of what's on your genetic scorecard or how many candles grace your birthday cake, every day presents an opportunity to fine-tune your health and well-being through the cadence of your habits and the harmony of your thoughts.

In this chapter, we'll explore the captivating world of epigenetics and uncover the profound impact that lifestyle choices can have on the expression of our genes.

Epigenetics is an intriguing science that reveals the interplay between our genes and our lifestyle. It explores how your choices can reshape the way your genes perform on the grand stage of your health and well-being.

This understanding is fundamental to embracing the path to becoming a vibrant sage. When I began preparing for my first marathon in 2008, I had no inkling of the genetic treasure hidden within me—a natural inclination for endurance and long-distance running. The adventure began in late February, with a soft blanket of snow shimmering in the early morning light. Our inaugural training run covered a humble four miles, a distance I had tackled only once in my distant past. The air was charged with anticipation as fellow runners, many of them new to the sport, united with a common purpose: raising funds for Team in Training and the Leukemia & Lymphoma Society. The first two miles were a downhill descent. They felt effortless, which filled me with exhilaration. However, the final two miles tested my resolve; I oscillated between brisk walking and brief bursts of running, eventually completing the four miles in fifty-five minutes. That triumphant moment ignited an unwavering determination within me.

The next four months of training pushed me to the brink, with each session demanding even more miles and leaving me physically and mentally exhausted. There were days when I felt utterly beaten down, questioning my decision to train for the marathon. Negative thoughts crept in, suggesting I might be too old, too out of shape for this challenge. But then I would remember the kids we were running for—those brave warriors fighting against cancer. They were our heroes, and I couldn't let them down. In moments of doubt and fatigue, their strength became my driving force, a powerful reminder that something greater than myself was propelling me forward. Those four months seemed to pass in the blink of an eye, and before I knew it, I was standing at the starting line in San Diego on that early June morning, ready to tackle my very first marathon.

The atmosphere was electric, a surge of excitement coursing through the runners and the cheering crowd alike. Those first ten miles breezed by as effortlessly as a light morning jog. I found myself alongside two teammates, our conversation spanning topics from running to the complexities of marriage and, yes, even into the fun realms of sex and more. Laughter and camaraderie filled the air.

But as we approached mile fifteen, I sensed a gradual slowdown in my pace. Remarkably, my teammates refused to leave my side, their unwavering support a testament to the bond we had forged during our training. By mile eighteen, I finally mustered the words to encourage them to go ahead without me, assuring them that I would meet them at the finish line.

On the distant horizon, the striking San Diego skyline loomed like the mythical Land of Oz. Fatigue coursed through my body, but the determination to finish, even if I had to walk, burned brightly within me. The relentless sun hung high overhead, casting scorching heat upon the pavement; it felt as if we were making a pilgrimage through a furnace. Doubt crept in. Was this the notorious "wall" I had heard about? That's when it happened—a group of Elvis impersonators, complete with a portable boombox, surged past me. Now, I had never been a devoted Elvis fan, but the infectious music filled me with renewed vigor and infused me with the energy I needed to keep going.

My legs began to cramp, and my resolve wavered, but I refused to yield. One step, then another. The finish line beckoned, and in just a little over five hours, I crossed it. Tears swelled in my eyes—not tears of pain or discomfort, but tears of pure, unadulterated joy. I had achieved the unimaginable. A mere four months prior, I struggled to complete a four-mile run, yet now I stood victorious after conquering the daunting 26.2 miles. The physical toll was par for the course, expected, and a few days of rest and recovery would be my well-earned reward.

Unlocking the Harmony between Genetic Predisposition and Epigenetics

As I reflected on that remarkable day, it dawned on me that my marathon journey was a perfect example of genetic predisposition and epigenetics working in harmony. My genes might have given me the potential, but it was my lifestyle choices, determination, and the unwavering support of my teammates that enabled me to transform that potential into a triumphant reality. It was a testament to the incredible power we hold over our genetic destiny. We can orchestrate our wellness by making conscious decisions that harmonize our genes and epigenetics and create beautiful melodies of vitality and achievement.

But genes alone do not dictate our destiny. While my DNA provided the first spark of potential, it was my lifestyle choices that either stoked the fires of my abilities or extinguished them. At the peak of my running journey, I neglected the importance of balance. Rest became a foreign concept, and proper nutrition took a backseat to my demanding schedule. I believed that my body would prevail over any challenge.

However, the harsh realities of life eventually caught up with me. The chronic cramping in my legs was not confined to race days; it invaded my sleep. Midday fatigue became a frequent companion. My memory faltered, and I struggled to follow directions at work. Yet, I remained oblivious to the message my body was screaming at me—to slow down, to rest.

At the age of fifty-three, I found myself at the crossroads of my health and fitness journey. My body's communication was now louder, more insistent than ever before. I pondered whether this was what aging truly entailed—aches, pains, mental lapses, and dwindling energy. Was I unknowingly wearing myself down, inadvertently causing harm to both body and mind?

In the realm of health and wellness, our march toward well-being extends far beyond just our physical actions and behaviors. It begins within the chambers of our own minds, where the genetic potential awaits its conductor. Imagine that our habits and lifestyle choices serve as the instruments, each capable of playing a unique note in the grand composition of our health. But the true maestro of this symphony is our mindset.

In the realm of epigenetics, we unlock the incredible potential of our minds to influence the very cells within our bodies. Real change, the kind that can profoundly change our health and well-being, starts with awareness—awareness of our thoughts, beliefs, and mental outlook. It is a shift in consciousness that sets in motion transformative changes at the cellular level. Just as a skilled conductor guides musicians to create beautiful and harmonious music, our thoughts and mental attitudes guide our genes to perform at their best.

Think of it this way: when we cultivate a positive and nurturing mindset, it's like we're instructing our genes to play a soothing and uplifting melody that reverberates through our bodies, influencing our cells to function optimally. On the contrary, if our mindset is negative or stress-ridden, our genes will produce dissonant chords, disrupting cellular harmony.

Ebbs and Flows in Energy, Vitality, Stamina, and Health

I have experienced these fluctuations firsthand—times when I felt unstoppable and others when I felt far from youthful.

The first time my body screamed at me was when I was in my midthirties, a mother of three with a demanding job and the usual responsibilities of adulthood. Slowly, my body started to send me signals—tingling in my fingers and toes, constant fatigue, and even episodes of graying vision. I pushed through it, fulfilling my obligations, until one day, I realized I couldn't ignore the signs any longer. It took a year of consultations with specialists, including one of New York City's top experts in conditions like multiple sclerosis. After reviews of my symptoms and history and countless tests, all returning negative results, I received an unexpected revelation—it was not a formal diagnosis but rather the shocking verdict that my physical problems were rooted in stress and emotional strain. It was an astonishing manifestation of epigenetics in action.

While I am profoundly grateful that it wasn't a more severe condition, it left me confused about how to effectively reduce stress. I tried meditation, but my racing thoughts made it seem impossible. Even a mere five-minute meditation session would leave me in tears. It was during this pivotal moment that I recognized my body was sending me a clear message: it was time to prioritize self-care, particularly during overwhelming and stressful times. This awakening marked the beginning of a journey where, for the next fifteen years, I listened to my body's cues, especially those related to emotional stress.

However, it is important to note that while I became attuned to my body's signals when it came to emotional stress, I later found myself neglecting these cues when it came to physical stress.

Embracing the Road to Vitality

Pause for a moment and consider: Have you ever brushed off minor aches or discomfort, telling yourself you'll deal with them later when you have more time? Have you faced relentless fatigue despite your best efforts to overcome it?

As we navigate through this riveting world of epigenetics, always remember—you hold the key to deciphering the blueprint of your health. Just as a builder consults architectural blueprints to craft harmonious structures, your awareness, mindfulness, and deliberate choices are the tools in this remarkable genetic construction.

Reclaiming your health and vitality may become more complex with age, but the crucial realization is this: you can enhance your well-being and energy, no matter your age. The blueprint of your health is still yours to interpret, with each choice you make adding to the architecture of your well-being. So embrace this journey with the confidence that, through your choices and mindset, you can build a structure of vitality that resonates throughout your life.

The question then becomes: What kind of design will you create for your well-being?

Awakening Your Inner Sage

Throughout life, our bodies undergo a magnificent transformation, a metamorphosis that unfolds regardless of whether we are fully prepared for it. Remember those teenage years when adulthood beckoned, a time marked by awkwardness and challenges? Did you ever ponder the habits you were forming and how they might shape your future health and vitality? As we move from childhood through adulthood, our bodies evolve, and it is crucial to reflect on how the choices we have made along the way influence our present state of well-being.

Possibly when you were younger, you could devour vast quantities of food without it leaving a trace on your physique. But now, even the mere sight of a donut adds extra pounds. Back in the day, you could play all day, free from the aches and pains that now come with a new exercise routine or prolonged periods of inactivity.

As we gracefully age, our genes undergo a transformation in their functioning, and this transformation is partly orchestrated by a wondrous process known as epigenetics. Picture it as a collection of instructions, notes, and highlights added to the pages of your DNA book. These annotations direct your cells, indicating which sections to read and when to read them.

With time, the markings in this book change. Some genes hush down like a soft volume on a radio, while others rise to prominence. This intricate dance between our genes and epigenetics influences our health and shapes the aging process.

Imagine your body's clock ticking at its unique pace, figuring out your biological age, which may differ from your chronological one. The good news is that your lifestyle choices can slow down the aging process, preserving your vibrancy.

So, as the years gracefully unfold, your genes and epigenetics share a dance, and the choices you make in life play a significant role in choreographing this dance. By embracing self-care and making positive decisions, you can help your body age gracefully while basking in the glow of enduring health and vitality.

As we move toward awakening your vibrant sage, let's look at the three key pillars of self-care that play a vital role in shaping your epigenetic health: minimizing chronic stress, consuming nourishing nutrition, and embracing movement.

1. **Minimize Stress:** In ancient times, stress was a vital survival mechanism, alerting us to potential dangers. If a lion or bear lurked nearby, your body's stress response prepared you for swift action. Thankfully, modern society seldom

thrusts us into such life-threatening situations where we need constant vigilance to survive.

2. **Nutrition That Nourishes:** You've heard the saying "You are what you eat," but let us expand that to "You are what your body digests and absorbs." During your youth, you might have indulged in donuts and pizza without immediate consequences. However, as you age, your dietary choices influence your epigenetic health. Forget the calorie count; it's the quality and variety of your food that truly matter. Embrace real, unprocessed foods that nurture your epigenetic well-being and bid adieu to chemical-laden, sugary, and unhealthy fare.

3. **Movement for Life:** Exercise is akin to a miracle elixir that profoundly influences your genes and cells. It can awaken genes linked to muscle growth and energy metabolism while silencing those associated with inflammation. Your choices for physical activity can significantly sway your epigenetic health, shaping how your genes are expressed and nurturing your overall well-being.

The Ever-Evolving Journey of Well-Being

In my thirties, life was a whirlwind of responsibilities. Career ambitions, raising a family, and managing daily chaos left little room for self-care. I was constantly on the move, juggling multiple roles, and my well-being often took a back seat. My body sent subtle signals—fatigue, aches, and occasional moments of anxiety—but I brushed them aside, thinking I could power through.

Fast-forward to my fifties, and the tune had changed. Life had shifted, and so had my body. The energetic, resilient me of the past started showing signs of wear and tear. Those whispers of discomfort in my thirties had grown into persistent aches, fatigue that no longer vanished with a good night's sleep, and the undeniable realization that my body was speaking louder than ever. It was a wake-up call—a reminder that well-being is not a one-time effort but an evolving journey. The priorities that once consumed my life had evolved, and so had my well-being needs. It was time to tune in, listen closely to the messages my body was sending, and adapt.

This is a journey we all take as we face different chapters and seasons of life. The key is not just in hearing your body's signals but in understanding how they change over time. Your story may be different, but the essence is still the same: we must continuously evaluate and tap into our well-being, for it evolves just as we do.

Conclusion

In this chapter, I took you on a fascinating journey into the depths of your body, exploring its intricate language and the profound impact of epigenetics. You learned that your body is constantly communicating with you, offering valuable insights into your well-being. As you reflect on your experiences and those I shared, you can begin to see the incredible potential that lies within you to shape your health trajectory.

In Part Two, we'll explore the five foundational pillars of optimal well-being more profoundly:

BREATH • MOVEMENT • NUTRITION • SLEEP • PURPOSE

These pillars are the foundational elements of becoming a vibrant sage. Understanding them deeply will offer insights into your well-being and help you identify areas for habit adjustments.

We'll examine these five pillars, guided by the wisdom and experiences of experts who have navigated their own challenges, learned to listen to their bodies, and made transformative changes, all while recognizing the profound influence epigenetics has on our well-being.

As we progress, always remember that your body is your most profound teacher, continuously offering valuable lessons if you are willing to listen. The path to becoming a vibrant sage awaits you.

Are you ready to explore the first pillar in this transformative journey and discover the profound impact of breath on your well-being?

PART TWO

Foundation for Arousing Health & Happiness— The Five Pillars

CHAPTER TWO

Foundation for Arousing Health & Happiness—
The Five Pillars

CHAPTER 4

PILLAR ONE

EMBRACING YOUR BREATH, YOUR POWER SOURCE

*Truly, it is Life (prana)that shines forth in all things!
Understanding this, one becomes a knower.*
—Swami Krishnananda, *The Mundaka Upanishad*

What do you think is the most fundamental thing you need to sustain life? "Water" is typically the immediate answer, given the constant reminders to hydrate, hydrate, hydrate. But what if I told you it is something even more essential, something often overlooked despite its profound influence on our vitality?

You may have already guessed the answer: it's air, or, more precisely, oxygen. Yet consider for a moment if you hadn't known the title of this chapter—what would have come to mind?

While breathing is an automatic bodily function, something we do without conscious thought, it is crucial to recognize that this life-sustaining act, when optimized, possesses tremendous power and is a vital part of vibrant aging. Have you ever taken a moment to reflect on the significance of your breath and its potential impact on your overall health?

Discovering the Power of Your Breath

As a seasoned speech pathologist, I had a wealth of knowledge about the intricate science of respiration, primarily in the context of speech. My academic training had equipped me with a deep understanding of the vital role breath played in articulation and vocalization. However, it was a chance encounter with Sam, a voice client I had the privilege to work with in the mid-1990s, whose life was profoundly affected by his breathing struggles, that would shatter my preconceived notions and reveal the extraordinary power hidden within our breath. Through his story and the science behind it, you'll see how something as fundamental as your breath can shape your health and happiness.

Breath is not just a tool for speech; it's a key to vitality and well-being. Beyond its fundamental importance for speech, I soon realized that our breath held the very foundation of our well-being—a revelation that would reshape not only my professional journey but also my personal understanding of life's vitality.

But before we dive into Sam's story, take a moment to consider your relationship with your breath. How often do you think about the way you breathe? How might your breath influence your well-being? Keep these questions in mind as we uncover the incredible potential that lies within your breath.

Sam's Journey: From Breathless to Reborn

Sam, a robust man in his midsixties with a striking white beard, bore a resemblance to Santa Claus. Beneath that jolly exterior, however, lay a two-year struggle that transcended his physical appearance. For Sam, breathing had become an ordeal. There were moments when he fought to complete a sentence, gasping for air as if it were slipping through his fingers. His voice had a strangled quality, but it was those unexpected bouts of breathlessness that haunted him the most. Sam confided that his greatest fear was blacking out while driving and potentially harming others. In the preceding two years, Sam had sought answers from a multitude of doctors, yet no one could pinpoint the root cause of his voice and breathing challenges. Finally, he found himself in the office of an otolaryngologist, or an ear, nose, and throat specialist, who, after a thorough examination, referred him to a speech pathologist for voice therapy.

Voice therapy was my passion at the time, and I marveled at the incredible power of the human voice. It is the art of transforming puffs of air into meaningful sounds, crafting them into words, and weaving them into the tapestry of human speech. Did you know that the sound of air passing through vocal cords is akin to the soft hiss of air escaping a balloon? The magic happens when that air finds its way into the throat, mouth, and nose, shaping itself into the language we understand.

As I conducted his evaluation, he was remarkably friendly and talkative. He shared the emotional toll of the past two years and how his struggles with speech and breathing had infiltrated every aspect of his life. It was a period where he'd lost hope, and he longed for the days when speaking and breathing came naturally. Armed with a diagnosis of spasmodic dysphonia and a referral for therapy, Sam was anxious yet hopeful that he could finally reclaim his life.

After gathering his background history, I conducted an oral motor evaluation to assess the movement and strength of his tongue, lips, and jaw. While his physical faculties were well within normal limits, one peculiarity stood out—a mild white film on his tongue, often a sign of dehydration. Sam confessed that he rarely drank beverages, with coffee being his beverage of choice throughout the day. Although we may occasionally experience the sensation of a dry mouth or a tongue uncomfortably sticking to the roof of our mouth, we often don't recognize how it can impede our ability to speak.

My next step was to look into the mechanics of his breathing and speech. It was here that the significance of breath became even more apparent. As I watched his breathing pattern at rest, a pattern marked by limited movement in his abdominal and chest areas, I could not help but think about the profound impact of something so seemingly ordinary.

Take a moment now to observe your breath. Do your abdominal area and chest gently rise and fall with each breath? This simple act, something we do unconsciously on average twenty thousand times each day, holds the key to our well-being and vitality—a fact that Sam's journey would soon underscore.

Next, I assessed Sam's breath support for speech—a critical aspect of his vocal challenges. I asked him to take a deep inhalation and then utter an extended "ah" sound for as long as possible. What unfolded during this exercise was both surprising and illuminating. His performance fell well below the typical ranges, which usually span between twenty-five to thirty-five seconds for men and fifteen to twenty-five seconds for women. However, what truly caught my attention was the uniqueness of his breathing pattern. As he inhaled deeply, he instinctively sucked his stomach in, creating an inward pull. Yet when it came to the exhalation phase, as he sustained the "ah" sound, he did something quite remarkable—he released his abdomen, allowing it to expand. It was a reverse breathing pattern, a breathing pattern unfamiliar to me.

Try it for yourself—take a deep breath while consciously sucking in your stomach, and then try to produce an "ah" sound for as long as you can. You will quickly realize the challenge of this inverted approach.

Normally, the act of inhaling causes the lungs to expand, prompting the chest and abdominal areas to rise as they create space for incoming air. This reservoir of air then fuels both speech and regular breathing. Conversely, a reverse breathing pattern restricts the flow of air into the lungs, diminishing the oxygen supply to the body and its cells. The consequences? Lightheadedness, irregular breathing, and a strained, strangled quality in one's voice.

Sam's evaluation unearthed several critical findings:
- A reverse breathing pattern
- Shallow breathing at rest and during speech
- A strangled vocal quality
- Significant dehydration

His treatment plan included voice therapy sessions twice a week, along with a dedicated focus on relearning proper breathing techniques and addressing the issue of dehydration. Yet there was a more profound revelation lurking beneath the surface of his challenges.

It became clear that Sam's struggles were not solely rooted in his physical condition. The combined effects of dehydration and insufficient airflow during breathing had triggered his alarming blackouts. He was not receiving adequate oxygen—an unsettling revelation for anyone. And his growing anxiety and fear concerning breathing difficulties compounded his ordeal.

Have you ever seen the shifts in your breathing patterns when anxiety or stress begin to influence you?

After two months of dedicated, intensive therapy, Sam experienced a transformation that bordered on the miraculous. Breathing became second nature to him once more, and the specter of breathlessness, which had haunted him for years, gradually faded.

Sam's journey is a profound reminder that simple changes can yield monumental benefits. It reinforced the notion that addressing a person's well-being involves more than just isolating a particular issue. The sum of our physical, mental, and emotional well-being is undeniably greater than the individual parts.

Most importantly, his story emphasized a fundamental truth—that the breath that sustains our life also lays the foundation for our voice and, by extension, our entire existence. This revelation would reverberate throughout my own exploration into the extraordinary connection between breath, well-being, and vibrant aging.

Sam is a testament to the power of transformation, expressed beautifully in his heartfelt testimonial, a keepsake I cherish to this day. It read, "The changes in my life are beyond my wildest hopes. I once again have a life."

Sam's triumphant journey revealed a universal truth: the extraordinary potential hidden within our breath, a facet often overlooked and taken for granted. This revelation is just the beginning of our exploration of the five pillars of vibrant aging, with the power of breath as our first stepping stone.

Sam's experience and the insights gained serve as a powerful reminder of how seemingly minor changes can lead to profound benefits. Through Sam, we see that our breath, often overlooked, holds the key to unlocking the potential for a life of vibrant well-being.

As we continue with this pillar, keep the profound wisdom of Sam's journey close to heart, for it holds invaluable lessons.

Alongside the transformative power of breath, his story becomes a guiding light on our path toward becoming vibrant sages, inspiring us to create a life brimming with vitality, wisdom, and enduring well-being.

Behind the Power of Breathing for Health and Vibrancy

According to Physiopedia.com, breathing affects all body systems; these systems, in turn, influence breathing. Optimal breathing patterns help support homeostasis, but when disrupted, significant issues can arise.[2]

Imagine that the power to unlock your body's full potential lies within something as simple and automatic as your breath. Science has revealed that breathing not only sustains life but profoundly influences our overall well-being. In fact, it's intricately connected to the autonomic nervous system (ANS), a complex network that governs crucial bodily functions.

While we all breathe naturally, few of us are aware of the incredible power we hold within our breath. It's a power that can change not just our respiratory system but also our heart rate, digestion, stress levels, and even our state of mind.

In my academic training, I focused on the physiological aspects of the breath—its mechanics, impact on the respiratory and circulatory systems, and its role in speech production. However, this scientific perspective left little room for investigating the profound connection between the breath and the mind. It was not until I had the privilege of working with Sam that I stumbled

---

[2] Physio-Pedia, "The Science of Breathing Well," Physio-Pedia, accessed October 28, 2023, https://www.physio-pedia.com/The_Science_of_Breathing_Well.

Disclaimer: The above client is solely based on my experience and the results with this particular client. While this case had an impact on my recognizing the power of the breath and optimizing the breath, I am aware that there are NUMEROUS CAUSES for breathing difficulties. If you have any concerns related to your breathing, seek medical attention, just like Sam did. As stated above, he had seen many professionals who ruled out medical causes for his difficulty.

upon the transformative power of breath optimization. It took years for me to fully grasp the extent of its impact on daily life, and it became clear why Sam described the experience as feeling reincarnated.

The Fundamental Science of Breathing

Your autonomic nervous system (ANS) is a crucial part of your overall nervous system responsible for managing the essential, automatic functions of your body that keep you alive. These are processes that occur seamlessly, whether you're awake or asleep, without conscious thought.

The Autonomic Nervous System (ANS) consists of three systems:
1. **Parasympathetic nervous system,** which is often thought of as our "rest and digest system"
2. **Sympathetic nervous system,** which is thought of as our "fight or flight system"
3. **Enteric system,** which is an extensive system of neurons connected to the gastrointestinal tract

Even though our ANS controls our respiratory system, our breath and how we breathe have a tremendous impact on other parts of the ANS, including heart rate and blood pressure.

While our respiratory system, like all physiological systems, is inherently intricate, I've streamlined the complexities to give you a more accessible understanding of your breath and, more importantly, the influence you can exert over it. Nonetheless, grasping the fundamentals remains pivotal.

The respiratory system consists of three distinct parts:
1. **The airway,** which consists of your nose, sinuses, mouth, throat, windpipe, and bronchial tubes. Think of this as the passage of the breath to and from the lungs.

2. **Lungs and blood vessels,** which form a complex and integrated system that is responsible for breathing in oxygen and then exchanging it with carbon dioxide. This exchange takes place in the capillaries.
3. **Muscles and bones,** which consist of the ribs and diaphragm, which is a strong wall of muscle that separates your chest cavity from the abdominal cavity.

Professionally, I was trained to assess all areas of the respiratory system related to phonation and speech. As you contemplate Sam's assessment, you can connect these three distinct parts of respiration. The ultimate connection is the production of vocal sounds, particularly speech.

In ancient times, breath was revered as the ultimate master key, holding the power to control both body and mind. As you read further, you will realize that it is the key to unlocking the full potential of your existence.

Breathing as the Bridge to Ancient Wisdom and Healing

Ancient wisdom believed in a "vital principle" coursing through the body, known as qi in China and prana in Hinduism. These cultures recognized respiration as a manifestation of this profound internal breath.[3] Philo of Alexandria, a renowned healer and philosopher around the time of Christ, emphasized the healing potential of the breath, saying, "All healing of the being is done through the breath. It was seen as the path to harmonizing the soul within the body, releasing tensions, blockages, and resistances, and opening the door to Creative Intelligence."[4]

---

[3] Christophe André, "Proper Breathing Brings Better Health," Scientific America, January 15, 2019, accessed March 24, 2024, https://www.scientificamerican.com/article/proper-breathing-brings-better-health.

[4] Margot Borden, "The Healing Power of the Breath," Psychology Everywhere, accessed January 4, 2024, https://psychologyeverywhere.com/articles/the-healing-power-of-breath.

Bridging Ancient Wisdom with Modern Science for Breath's Optimal Power

Breathing is essential to sustaining life. Various factors affect how long an adult can survive without oxygen, but on average, "between thirty and one hundred and eighty seconds of oxygen deprivation, you may lose consciousness. At the one-minute mark, brain cells begin dying. At three minutes, neurons suffer more extensive damage, making lasting brain damage more likely. At five minutes, death becomes imminent. At ten minutes, permanent brain damage occurs, and after fifteen minutes, survival is nearly impossible."[5]

Four fascinating insights into how your breath affects your body and cells that highlight the importance of continuous, mindful breathing are:

1. **Cells Crave Oxygen:** Every cell in your body needs oxygen for energy and growth. When you inhale, your blood absorbs oxygen and distributes it to every nook and cranny of your body. This fuels your cells, helping them carry out their daily tasks with vigor.

2. **Detoxifying with Exhalations:** But it's not just about inhaling oxygen. Exhalation plays a vital role too. Did you know that approximately 70 percent of the waste your body produces is eliminated through your breath?[6] That's right—carbon dioxide is the trash your cells want to get rid of.

3. **Exchanging Gases:** It has been estimated that when you inhale, the air contains roughly 21 percent oxygen and

---

[5] Spinal Cord Team, "What You Need to Know About Brain Oxygen Deprivation," Spinal Cord, April 26, 2021, accessed November 5, 2023, https://www.spinalcord.com/blog/what-happens-after-a-lack-of-oxygen-to-the-brain.

[6] Alina Bradford, "Lungs: Facts, Function and Diseases," Live Science, February 1, 2018, accessed October 30, 2023, https://www.livescience.com/52250-lung.html.

only 0.4 percent carbon dioxide. Exhale, and you are expelling 16.4 percent oxygen and a whopping 4.4 percent carbon dioxide.[7] Why? Because your cells are devouring the oxygen and producing carbon dioxide as a byproduct.

4. **Breathing by the Numbers:** On average, you may take anywhere between seventeen thousand and twenty-two thousand breaths per day, inhaling the equivalent of thirteen pints of air every minute. That's a lot of oxygen and a lot of opportunities for your cells to thrive.

Stress, Cognition, and the Breath

Stress places our body and mind in a state of hyperarousal. This system is often referred to as "fight or flight." Ever notice how your breath changes when you're stressed? Shallow, rapid breaths are your body's way of preparing for action. It's the sympathetic nervous system at work, getting you ready to fight or flee. The system is there to protect you during periods of "danger," when you need to be on high alert, and then once the danger is over, it goes back into the parasympathetic state of rest and digest. Yet today, we live in a world where chronic stress is on the rise.

According to Paleo Stress Management, 55 percent of American adults report being stressed during the day. This is 20 percent higher than the global average![8] The result is an increase in chronic health problems and mental health struggles.

Previously, I shared the impact of holding your breath for minutes, with you passing out by three minutes. While this is an extreme example, even holding your breath for just a few seconds can have a detrimental impact on your focus and attention. Your

---

7   "Gasses: We Breathe In and Breathe Out," Byjus, accessed November 30, 2023, https://byjus.com/biology/composition-gases-breathe/#:~:text=When%20we%20 exhale%2C%20the%20 composition,and%204.4%25%20of%20carbon%20dioxide.

8   Alex Reijnierse, "Stress Statistics: Infographics Of Modern-Day Stress," Paleo Stress Management, April 5, 2024, accessed April 11, 2024, https://paleostressmanagement.com/stress-statistics-infographics.

brain, like any other part of your body, requires fuel to function effectively, and that fuel is oxygen.

Research in this area has gone beyond the act of respiration itself and examined how your breath communicates with your brain. Numerous studies have found that slow, steady breaths significantly enhance your ability to maintain focus and attentiveness. Conversely, a shallow breathing pattern, or those moments when we unconsciously hold our breath for brief intervals, can gradually erode our ability to concentrate and pay attention.

Did you know . . .

Your Breath Can Be a Stress-Reducer: The good news is you have a tool at your disposal, twenty-four seven! Control of your breath. While it cannot completely remove the stress, it can have a positive impact on the automatic nervous system. It can calm your body, lower blood pressure, clear your mind, and detoxify your body.

The Health Benefits of Mindful Breathing: Besides their role in managing stress, mindful breathing practices have shown remarkable effects on overall health. Studies reveal that these practices are effective in combating anxiety, depression, and stress. Even a single session can significantly reduce blood pressure, offering an instant sense of calm.

There's an Emotional-Breath Connection: It's fascinating how your emotions can alter your breath. When stress hits, you may find your breath becoming shallow and rapid. The reverse is also true—by taking charge of your breath, you can influence your emotions positively.

Practical Tips for Better Breathing: Take a few slow, deep breaths right now. Notice how it calms you down instantly. That is the power of your breath in action.

So there you have it. Your breath isn't just the autopilot of life; it is your key to vibrant health and well-being. Next, I'll introduce you to some practical exercises and techniques that will empower you to fully harness the transformative potential of your breath. What makes it even more exciting is that our understanding of the science behind your breath's impact on mental health and well-being is still in its infancy. The road ahead promises new discoveries and insights that can shape the way you experience life, health, and vitality.

Unlocking the Power of Your Breath

Most of the time, breathing happens naturally, without much thought. But this simple act has incredible potential to improve both your physical and emotional well-being. Your breath is a potent tool waiting to be harnessed for your best health, no matter your age.

Think of your breath as a hidden biohack to unlock your vibrancy! To fully tap into this power, it's crucial to recognize when your breathing pattern is shallow or suboptimal and understand how it can change your overall health.

Shallow Breathing—A Silent Saboteur

Shallow breathing, characterized by minimal airflow into the lungs and the use of chest muscles rather than the diaphragm, disrupts the delicate balance of oxygen and carbon dioxide in your body. This imbalance can lead to increased blood pressure and heart rate. Shallow breathing can sneak into your life for several reasons, such as habits, anxiety, stress, fear, or even respiratory conditions like asthma.

Have you ever noticed how your breathing patterns change when you're engrossed in reading emails? Yes, it's a real phenomenon known as "email apnea." Your body responds to the stress and urgency of emails by altering your breath, often without you realizing it.

Biohack Your Vibrancy—Time to Breathe!

Let's put this new knowledge into action with a simple exercise:

Exercise 1: The Breathing Check

1. Place one hand on your abdomen and the other on your chest.
2. Just breathe normally for thirty seconds. Pay attention to your chest and abdomen.

Did you feel your abdominal or chest area expanding?
Did you notice the cool air entering your nostrils?
How did it feel?

Exercise 2: Mindful Breathing

1. Take a slow, deep breath in for four counts, feeling the cool air in your nostrils.
2. Hold it for four counts.
3. Exhale for four counts.
4. Repeat this process four to six times (about one minute).

Are you feeling a little more relaxed?

Understanding Your Breath

As you practice these exercises, focus on the rise and fall of your abdominal area. With each inhalation, imagine your lungs expanding like a balloon, causing your abdomen to rise. This diaphragmatic activation is a key part of best breathing.

Nostril Breathing—The Art of Mindful Breath

Breathing through your nose has some surprising benefits. It warms up the air and acts as a filter, keeping pollutants and viruses at bay. Plus, it releases nitric oxide molecules, which play roles in health and even sexual stimulation. As you inhale and exhale through your nose, notice how the temperature of the air changes.

By the time you have completed six to eight mindful breaths, you might feel more relaxed and focused. Your breath holds the key to unlocking a world of vitality and well-being, and we're just scratching the surface of what it can do for you.

Breath and Becoming a Vibrant Sage

It's easy to take our breath for granted, since it's an automatic function that keeps us alive. But your breath is not only the foundation of life; it's also the cornerstone of vibrancy and well-being.

As we age, our bodies change in many ways, and our lung health is no exception. Our once-strong respiratory muscles gradually weaken, making us more susceptible to illness and reducing the vitality of every cell in our body.

Breathing is no longer something we can afford to overlook or take for granted. Instead, we must actively embrace the power of our breath, nurture it, and make it a cornerstone of our journey to vibrant aging.

Making the Unconscious Conscious

Breathe in, breathe out—it is something you do without even thinking about it. That is why Pillar One is breath!

But what if I told you that your breath holds the key to unlocking a world of vibrant well-being, and all it takes is a little awareness?

My client Sam serves as a compelling example. He was breathing, but his unconscious breathing pattern was silently sabotaging his health. How or why he developed this pattern is a mystery we may never solve. However, once he gained insight into the power of conscious breathing—slow, deep inhales followed by gradual, mindful exhales—his life transformed within a few weeks.

A vibrant life is all about waking up each day with boundless energy, and guess what? Your breath plays a starring role in this grand production. Even when life serves up distractions and conflicts, your breath is still a steadfast, cost-free ally, helping you feel better from the inside out.

Using Your Breath to Optimize Health, Happiness, and Vitality

Now that we've explored the incredible potential of conscious breathing, let's put this knowledge into action. The journey to health, happiness, and vitality through improved breathing begins with a simple yet transformative challenge: the Seven-Day Daily Breath Awareness Challenge.

Before you dismiss this as just another routine, let me assure you, this challenge is different. It will not consume your time, it will not cost a dime, and it's astonishingly simple. You have absolutely no excuse to skip it!

The Seven-Day Breath Challenge

Your mission, should you choose to accept it, is to dedicate just one minute each day for seven days to practicing conscious breathing. You are free to pick any time that suits your schedule—it's that flexible. Place your hand gently on your heart or chest and let your breath guide you. Inhale slowly, exhale mindfully, and pay close attention to each breath.

Start Your Day with a Deep, Mindful Breath

One surefire way to ensure you follow through with this daily practice is to kick-start your mornings with it. Here is a simple three-step routine that takes just a minute but can set a profoundly positive tone for your entire day:

1. Inhale deeply, allowing life-giving air to fill your lungs. As you exhale, relish the simple joy of another day to live. It might sound deceptively simple, but trust me, this act holds immense power.
2. Take a few more deep breaths while reflecting on something you're genuinely grateful for. It could be a loving relationship, a personal achievement, or the beauty of nature outside your window.
3. Inhale deeply once again, and as you exhale, say to yourself, "I am . . . " followed by a positive thought or intention. For example, "I am a loving mother," "I am strong," or "I am grateful for another day."

The two most powerful words in the world are "I am . . . " Your thoughts and intentions have a direct impact on your life. This simple yet profound morning ritual can significantly boost your well-being and add an extra layer of positivity to your life.

So, are you up for the challenge? I really encourage you to do this, starting with just one minute a day. The power to optimize your life through breath is within your grasp, just waiting to be harnessed.

Breathing for a Vibrant Day! Check-Ins throughout the Day

In the hustle and bustle of life, we often find ourselves juggling countless responsibilities and battling stress at every turn. Amid all this chaos, it's easy to forget the vital connection between our breath and our emotional well-being. But fret not; here are some practical ways to check in with your breath and manage stress throughout the day.

Set Breath Reminders

Consider setting a timer or an hourly alarm to remind you to check in on your breath. It's a simple yet effective way to ensure you're keeping a healthy breathing pattern. When that chime goes off, take a moment to focus on your breath. Inhale deeply, exhale mindfully, and feel the stress melt away.

Embrace Breath Apps

In our tech-savvy world, there is an app for everything, including monitoring your breathing. Many apps are readily available to help you track your breath and provide real-time feedback. These nifty tools can alert you when your breathing becomes shallow or erratic, nudging you back toward calm and balance.

Breathe Mindfully While Texting and Emailing

Most of us spend a massive part of our day glued to our screens, whether texting or checking emails. Turn these mundane moments into opportunities for mindful breathing. Take a pause, close your eyes for a second if you can, and take a few deep breaths. It's a minor change that can have an enormous impact on your stress levels.

Find Your Laughter Source

Laughter truly is the best medicine. Whenever you need a quick pick-me-up, find something that makes you laugh—a funny video, a silly friend, or even a hilarious meme. Laughter not only lightens your mood; it also encourages natural, deep breathing and releases those feel-good endorphins.

Meditate for Inner Peace

When stress starts to build up, take a moment to meditate. It doesn't require hours of silence—even a few minutes can work wonders. Close your eyes, take a few deep, intentional breaths, and let go of the chaos around you. Focus on your breath, and with each exhale, imagine stress and tension melting away.

Your breath is your faithful companion throughout the day. By incorporating these simple practices into your routine, you can utilize the power of your breath to manage stress and maintain your vibrant well-being. So, why wait? Start checking in with your breath today and experience the transformative effects on your life.

Interview with a Certified Breathwork Professional

Embarking on a Journey of Discovery

When I began writing this book in 2021, I had no idea of what lay ahead. As a speech pathologist, I thought I knew a lot about the intricacies of breath, but I was in for a revelation. While doing research for this book, I stumbled upon the vast and fascinating world of breathwork, a world that I had previously overlooked.

It wasn't until the fall of 2022 that I made a remarkable discovery. There are dedicated teachers who specialize in breathwork—individuals who have made it their life's mission to explore the profound impact of breath on our well-being.

My curiosity led me to a variety of breathwork programs and teachers, and it was during this search that I began my life-changing journey. Among the many excellent programs available, one stood out—the Breathwork Instructor Course, presented by Michaël Bijker, the visionary founder of Yogalap.

Immersing myself in breathwork was transformative. It opened my eyes to the immense potential of the breath, beyond what I had ever imagined as a speech pathologist. As I completed the course, I felt a deep desire to share his wisdom with my readers.

So I reached out to Michaël, hoping he would agree to an interview. Fortunately, he graciously accepted, and what follows is a captivating conversation that will provide you with fresh insights and a profound appreciation for the power of breath.

Introducing Michaël Bijker: A Leading Voice in Breathwork

Michaël has earned his place as a distinguished figure in the world of breathwork. With a decade of dedicated study and practice, he has transformed the lives of thousands of individuals across the globe. Becoming a certified eight-hundred-hour teacher, coupled with his yoga therapy certification, has empowered Michaël to share the profound benefits of conscious breathing with a vast and growing community.

As a testament to his expertise and the effectiveness of his teachings, Michaël has guided more than one hundred thousand individuals to improve their mental and physical well-being. His courses and programs have resonated with people from around the world, helping them tap into the incredible potential of their breath.

In the following interview, Michaël shares his story, insights, and the transformative power of breathwork. Prepare to be inspired by his wisdom as he relays the secrets of breathwork and its incredible potential for enhancing our lives.

Q: Share a little information about yourself for our readers.

I teach people how to connect with their breath, energy, mind, and nervous system to calm and to harmonize everything. Living a life of joy, peace, and purpose, you need these tools. With them, you experience life to be in a good state of mind and health.

And this really happens through breathing. I also help people with meditation, yoga, and qigong. Nowadays, more and more people are starting to realize how important it is to breathe well, to be able to calm down your own nervous system, or to energize your body . . . all these things. And it happens through breathing.

Q: What was your journey to breathwork or to recognizing the power of the breath?

Since I was young, I have always been extremely interested in spirituality and meditation. I noticed that breathing plays such an important role in many diverse types of meditation.

When you can control your breathing, it is like a doorway to the subconscious mind and your ability to control your mind.

Q: Tell me about how you used breathing to help you with eczema.

When I was younger, I suffered from eczema. The doctors gave me creams, pills, and all sorts of things to use on the outside to heal something that comes from the inside. I learned then, thank God, the beautiful practice of the calm and strong breathing techniques that could be used to heal from the inside. I came to the art of breathwork not only to heal physically and mentally but also to learn the truth about life on a spiritual level.

Q: Why do you think breathing helps with eczema?

My struggle with eczema led me to a Chinese medicine doctor. He viewed eczema as burn marks—to him, it meant the body is too hot. The brain and the mind were using too much energy, and it was heating up my whole nervous system.

I thought to myself, well, that is interesting. So, I started looking more into that—how to cool down the mind. Breathing helped tremendously, and slowly I healed.

Q: Did your experience of discovering how to ultimately cure your eczema have an impact on how you view health?

Lots of things in life, especially diseases, can push you in a certain direction to take certain types of actions. But this new discipline was so hard for me, especially because I was young. It was difficult for me to sit still. I always wanted to be active and do things. My mind was like a wild animal, and I did not really know how to tame it.

If I had been healthy, I would be thinking, Why should I sit still? I could be doing a lot of things. But it was so difficult suffering from eczema. And I was also suffering from a restless mind. I remember suffering all day, and then at night I would wake up scratching my body. I was suffering, red all over, and my skin was broken everywhere.

I had to decide. I can keep doing what I am doing and experience suffering twenty-four seven, or I can make myself sit still twice a day, half an hour each time, and go through the suffering of a restless mind, learning how to just sit with it and calm it down—cool it down.

Once I discovered that calming my mind helped, I had to decide whether to continue to practice quieting my mind and the practice of breathing or live with a medium amount of suffering. I chose to get rid of the suffering. Over time, it got easier, and now it has become an incredibly beautiful practice that I love and enjoy—finding peace within.

Q: Many people have shared with me, "I can't meditate. There is no way I can calm my mind." I guess this is what is referred to as monkey mind? Could you share how breathing can help us quiet our minds?

First of all, the beautiful thing about breathing techniques is that they give you a tool. Without this tool, as you experienced, to sit still with your eyes closed and then try to meditate, your monkey mind does come up, and the harder you may try to calm it, the worse it may get.

You must give the mind something to do. For example, counting breaths can be a wonderful place to start. Slowing breathing while focusing on counting your breaths gives your mind something to do, which helps the entire nervous system calm down. And then over time, it gets easier.

Q: What about someone who says they simply do not have time to "do nothing" and to practice breathing or meditation?

First, you must ask yourself, How do I want to prioritize my lifetime? A lot of people find it easy to spend three hours a day scrolling through social media or watching the news, or to maybe also spend hours, nine hours of the day on a job, on their work, which is not really something they even feel is in line with their heart's desire.

For those who believe that they do not have time, I ask them: How do you prioritize your time? How important is your mental and physical health to you? Ideally, breathwork should be part of your day and just as important as your job, social media, or watching the news.

Q: I often tell my clients that optimizing their breath is a form of biohacking because it impacts every cell in their body. How

would you explain the importance of perfecting breath to perfect health? What is an easy explanation for people to understand?

If all the systems in your body—your endocrine system, hormones, nervous system, blood flow, and the cardiovascular system—are all balanced and working well, then your body can heal well, and it's not necessary to become sick. Also, your mind will be clear, and everything will be good and in balance.

With breath, you can harmonize and balance out these systems, especially with extraordinarily strong breathing. You can release certain hormones that are very activating—for example, adrenaline or cortisol. You can create certain neurons and release certain neurotransmitters in your brain. You can influence your own endocrine and nervous systems.

You can activate both the parasympathetic nervous system—the rest and digest part of the nervous system—and the sympathetic nervous system, which is the fight-or-flight mode. You can increase your heart rate or slow down your heart rate.

You can use your nervous system as a remote control for all the other systems in the body. You access it through breathing. Therefore, breathing gives you the opportunity to balance out, clear out, purify, or strengthen your body systems. And with these systems, you are a living being.

Q: Where should someone begin if they know nothing about breathwork and conscious breathing?

Start with the basics of breathing correctly—especially how to use your diaphragm. You can think of the diaphragm as the breathing muscle underneath the lung. It's a big muscle about the size of my hand. The diaphragm gets pushed down as you suck air into the lungs, which then pushes the belly out, and it releases as you exhale.

When a person sucks in their stomach to feel skinny, this can prevent a person from really perfecting or even using their diaphragm. It negatively affects breathing. Also, many people express that they have a lot of tension around the area of the heart. When this is the case, think of stress blocking emotions. This also negatively affects proper functioning of the blocks of this diaphragm muscle.

Consequently, people may find it really hard to breathe calmly and deeply because everything is stuck. People need to relearn how to breathe with their diaphragm muscle. They have to allow the belly to come out as they breathe in and release the breath out to make that breathing go deep again. Then they start to loosen up at the heart center, where there can be so much blocked emotion and stress. When they release that emotion and stress to open up the area, suddenly the whole nervous system goes into a different state, and it's a more peaceful state.

You become more accepting in the moment toward yourself when this happens. This is how you will be able to not just physically loosen up and open emotionally, but also loosen up on a deeper energetic and spiritual level as well.

Q: Is there a correlation between breathing and anxiety disorders?

There is a direct link between mental health and breathing. Think about very strong emotions, such as crying or laughing, and how your breathing changes. When we are relaxed, our breathing becomes deeper and calmer. When we are stressed out, the breathing becomes high up in the chest and noticeably short. Your breathing pattern changes with your emotional states and with your state of mind.

Q: Are you saying you can control the state of your emotions using your breath?

Once you can control your breathing, you can start to control your emotional state and your general state of mind. There's a direct correlation between the breath and the state of your nervous system, mind, and energetic state.

Q: How do you use your breath to optimize your body and mind? When did this whole concept start?

The practice of prana—breath, life force energy—is a beautiful ancient yogic breathing practice. It was used to clean out the body and purify the body and mind.

Q: What are some different breathing practices?

One of them is called Kapalabhati breaths, which are short pulsing breaths through the nose and then breathing with the belly, like contracting, releasing, contracting, releasing. It is a wonderful way to stimulate the flow of energy through the body to wake up and open up the whole energetic system.

When everything is a bit lethargic, like when the "fire" in your body is low, you can use this breathing technique to stimulate, unblock, and open. Think about how great you feel after laughing—more energized and alive. Some of the strong yogi breathing can be a wonderful tool to wake you up and feel amazing. However, it is also very important to calm down everything again with slow breathing.

Q: In your Breath of Life course, you taught us many different techniques. I look at them as a toolbox to help harmonize, open, and clear out the mind and the body.

Yes, it is a toolbox. Your body is the vessel through which you experience this life. We experience our whole life through our senses, our mind, and emotions. All these systems need to be in a best condition to make your life a greatest experience, right? Therefore, it is essential to have everything in a good state.

Here is an analogy. You are starting on a journey in your car, but it breaks down constantly. It starts to rain, but the wipers do not function properly, so you don't see clearly. When it gets dark, the lights don't function properly, and you can't see. The point is you have to get your car in a best state to travel nicely through life, right?

It's the same with this physical body we have, and breathing really helps. On the other hand, we have to remember that this life experience through the senses of the body is experienced by something which is beyond the mind, beyond the senses, which is the essence of our pure consciousness. The true self.

Breathing helps us remember what we are, to remember that even though this body is going to pass one day and even though all the things that we have now in this lifetime are things we are going to lose. There is something at the essence which is beyond that which is eternal and which is connected to the essence of creation. God's great spirit.

Q: I attended various trainings, including one featuring a brief yet intense three-minute consecutive breathing exercise. Surprisingly, tears streamed down my cheeks at the end, reminiscent of moments in yoga classes when I would also shed tears during the final resting pose, the corpse pose. It made me wonder: how does our breath have the power to release not only physical toxins but also what I believe are trapped emotions? What's the science behind this phenomenon?

Every experience, every emotion, all the memories are not only in the brain, right? Our brain is not just this area here in one location. It goes throughout the whole body. Your whole body is connected to the brain. Your whole body is one extensive network of nerve cells, neurons going through the whole body, right?

Every experience is somewhere in the cells of the body. It is stuck somewhere. We have created ways throughout our lives, exceptionally good mechanisms, not to feel any discomfort or not to get confronted with certain memories or emotions. There is an entire system that kind of blocks us from really experiencing these emotions, but this doesn't mean the emotions are not there. They are somewhere in our system.

As soon as we do certain types of breathing techniques, we start to massage out some of these tensions. They start to be released and come to the surface or come up through the doors of our awareness. When we do these breathing techniques, things start to come out. Things start to loosen up the defense mechanism of protecting those emotions from being experienced.

So, they start to release. And when we go through these experiences the right way, we can start to get them out of our system.

Crying is part of the subconscious, which we cannot control. As I mentioned at the beginning, the breath is the doorway. Breath is the tool, the remote control between the conscious and the subconscious. When we can start making that link, we bring the awareness into the subconscious and experience it all.

Q: Earlier, we said a good place for somebody to start is to just breathe properly. I discuss that in this book and suggest lying down so you can feel and see your abdominal area rising, maybe even placing a book or something on the belly. Beyond that, what would you recommend? Do most of us need somebody like you

to help us learn how to perfect our breath? Is that something we can get from yoga or just from meditating? What would be your advice?

It can be very helpful having somebody teach you the techniques like I'm doing in the Breathless Life course or online videos. But you don't have to. Start with awareness and taking little moments to begin to integrate breathwork into your daily life.

Maybe begin by taking a moment to place one hand on your belly and the other on your heart and simply take a few nice deep breaths. This can even be done first thing in the morning while you are waiting for your morning coffee or toast or even watching a bird. If you have a little moment, take some deep breaths, connect with your breathing system so that you start to reprogram your whole nervous system.

Q: What do you think they will get from that reprogramming—from their breath, from breathing properly?

First, they will start to feel more of a connection in their being, with their body and their mind. Then they will feel more grounded and present, more at home with being alive.

There is this disconnection between people and life, between the present moment here and now. This happens because a lot of people are constantly worrying about the future or dealing with a certain memory or constantly creating new ideas. And that disconnection results in anxiety, depression, various forms of stress, all kinds of things. So that is a particularly important thing to know.

On a deeper level, when we start to make more connection with our true self and live with less fear and stress, then the more aligned we become with what we truly want to do in life instead of what others expect from us or what our mind tells us how we should be or what we should be. But just living out of that desire to live, to give, and to flow is what changes our lives.

Wisdom and Insight from Michaël's Interview

Michaël's journey into breathwork and his deep understanding of its power to transform lives is truly inspiring. He has not only used breathwork to heal himself physically and mentally but has also found profound spiritual insights through this practice. His dedication to teaching others how to connect with their breath, energy, mind, and nervous system reflects his passion for helping people live healthier, more peaceful and purposeful lives.

Michaël emphasizes the importance of proper breathing as a tool for achieving our best health, both physically and mentally. He highlights how breathwork can harmonize and balance the body's systems, influence the nervous system, and improve our overall well-being. By controlling our breath, we can control our emotional states and our state of mind, making it a valuable tool for managing anxiety and stress.

He encourages us to prioritize our mental and physical health by incorporating breathwork into our daily lives. Michaël's teachings remind us that perfecting our breath is a form of self-care, akin to biohacking, that can affect every cell in our bodies. It's a powerful tool that helps us reconnect with our true selves and find peace and harmony in our lives.

Amid our busy lives, Michaël's advice to be available for breathwork and to prioritize our well-being is a reminder that we have the power to create positive change in our lives and, in turn, contribute to a more balanced and harmonious world. His words of wisdom encourage us to act and find joy, peace, and purpose through the practice of conscious breathing.

Overall, Michaël's insights and teachings on breathwork are a valuable resource for anyone looking to improve their physical, mental, and spiritual health.

Please see the Acknowledgments and Contact Information sections at the end of the book for more details about Michaël.

Breathing Life: Unveiling the Secrets of Vibrant Aging

In this chapter, we explored the transformative power of breath. We've learned that perfecting our breath is the cornerstone of vibrant living, and its significance only grows as we age. From ancient wisdom to innovative research, we unveiled the profound influence that conscious breathing can have on our physical and emotional well-being.

Through the stories of Sam, who regained his life through breathwork, and Michaël, who found relief from a persistent condition, we have seen the real-life impact of simple yet profound changes in our breath patterns.

Now, armed with the awareness of our breath's potential, let's move on to Pillar Two, movement. Just as our breath is the foundation of vitality, movement is the key to unlocking our physical potential and enhancing our strength, flexibility, and overall health. Get ready to learn how incorporating small, sustainable changes into our daily routines can synergize with our new understanding of breath, propelling us toward a life of vibrancy, purpose, and passion.

Have you ever considered that the way you breathe could hold the key to unlocking your untapped potential for a vibrant, purposeful, and healthier life?
Are you ready to take the first conscious breath toward a life filled with vitality and lasting well-being?

CHAPTER 5

PILLAR TWO

EMBRACING MOVEMENT, NO GYM REQUIRED

We do not stop playing because we grow old—we grow old because we stop playing.
— George Bernard Shaw

Picture an active life, one where you're brimming with energy, agility, and boundless vitality, all without the confines of a gym. We often associate fitness with strenuous workouts, elaborate equipment, and rigid routines. But what if I told you that the key to rejuvenating your body lies in a different approach, one that doesn't demand a gym membership or hours of sweat-soaked effort?

Just as children effortlessly explore the world with curiosity and grace through their movement, this chapter invites you to rediscover the art of fluid, everyday motion. Let's delve into the exhilarating world of movement, where no gym is needed, yet the rewards are endless. Just as enhancing your breath lays the foundation for vibrant aging, embracing the power of movement is the next step to becoming a vibrant sage. This is your path to unlocking the secret of vibrant aging through the joyous simplicity of movement.

Late Bloomer to Fitness Enthusiast: My Story of Transformation

I'll confess that I wasn't always the exercise enthusiast you might picture today. Despite holding a gym membership for most of my life, I just didn't resonate with the regimented exercise routines it often mandated. If anything, I found those structured workouts more of a chore than a source of joy—a sentiment many of you might relate to.

Back then, I enjoyed more spontaneous kinds of movement, like hiking, cycling, walking, or even running around while coaching my kids' youth soccer team. Those were the moments when I felt truly alive, not bound by rigid schedules or exercise machines.

Furthermore, in the hustle and bustle of my life, especially during my thirties and early to midforties, it became all too easy to place the demands of work and family above my own well-being.

In 2008, as I started on my fitness journey, becoming a certified personal trainer was not even on my radar. Little did I know that within five years, I would experience a profound transformation that not only reshaped my perspective but also set the course for inspiring others on their wellness journeys.

Over those five years, my relationship with the gym and structured workouts underwent a remarkable evolution. Initially, I found the workouts challenging, not necessarily delightful. But as time unfolded, my belief shifted, and I recognized the benefits they held for my overall health and vitality. Gradually, I developed a genuine appreciation for the gym, the art of movement, and the rich sense of wellness they brought.

This new enthusiasm for fitness, rooted in my love of the gym, led to a revelation. I had assumed that motivating older adults to embrace exercise would be effortless, fueled by my personal experience of its transformative power. I envisioned a similar experience for others, especially those in the golden years of their lives.

However, the reality was that not everyone shared my perspective, particularly as they aged. For many, exercise felt more like an obligation than a choice. It was then that I grasped the importance of cultivating intention behind movement, a process that takes time but becomes increasingly vital as we grow older. My transformation and my experiences with motivating others have taught me the profound power of setting intentions for movement and the invaluable well-being it brings as we age.

Did you ever think that how you feel about exercise might be in your DNA? It's a fascinating aspect of our genetic makeup—the genes associated with loving or, well, not-so-loving exercise.

As a personal trainer, I've been in the trenches, working tirelessly to motivate my clients to stick to their exercise routines. And let me tell you, it's been quite an endeavor. I have come to realize that not everyone wakes up excited to hit the gym. Some people simply tolerate it, while others, quite frankly, loathe it.

Whether you're someone who has always had a burning passion for exercise and loves going to the gym, or if the thought of formal workouts sends shivers down your spine, there's something remarkable we all share: the universal need for movement. It goes beyond the confines of gyms, weights, or treadmills. It's about the simple act of keeping your body in motion, every single day. What is truly incredible is that by embracing this movement, you unlock a hidden wellspring of boundless energy, enduring vitality, and unwavering health. No matter where you currently stand on the exercise spectrum, the road ahead promises something extraordinary.

In this chapter, we'll address the profound impact that movement has on becoming vibrant sages. We'll begin with discovering why our cells and our bodies need movement—why it is essential to integrate cardiovascular movement, strength training, balance, and flexibility into our daily activities.

Once the foundation has been set, I'll share stories of individuals who have harnessed the power of movement to transform their lives. These inspirational stories will illuminate the path to rewriting our own narratives and embracing movement as a conduit to vibrant aging. Through their experiences, we will uncover the wisdom and insights that can propel each of us toward becoming a vibrant sage.

The Power of Exercise: Energizing Your Cells for a Healthier You

Do you exercise solely for a toned physique or to shed those extra pounds? While those are valid reasons, there's a lot more going on beneath the surface when you work up a sweat. Let's dive into the fascinating world of cellular health and how exercise supercharges your cells.

Imagine your body is a bustling metropolis, and your cells are the hardworking citizens. At the heart of this bustling city are the mitochondria, often called the powerhouse of the cell. These tiny organelles are the key players responsible for converting the food you eat into energy. This energy, in the form of molecules known as adenosine triphosphate (ATP), fuels every cell, tissue, and organ in your body.

So, how does exercise fit into this picture? Well, it's the switch that turns these cellular powerhouses into overdrive. When you engage in physical activity, you activate your cells to produce more energy, and mitochondria get to work. They take in oxygen, break down nutrients, and churn out ATP, providing you with the vitality you need to conquer your day.

But exercise is not just about energy production; it's also about cellular respiration—a fancy term for your cells' ability to breathe and detoxify. Just as you consciously use your breath to calm your mind and reduce stress, cellular respiration needs exercise to kick into gear. Through exercise, your cells inhale oxygen, which is vital for energy production, and exhale toxins. This detox process creates space for newer, healthier cells to take the stage, keeping you youthful and vibrant, both physically and mentally.

So, how can you tap into this incredible cellular transformation? It's simpler than you might think. The Centers for Disease Control and Prevention (CDC) recommends one hundred and fifty minutes (or two hours and thirty minutes) of moderate cardiovascular exercise each week, coupled with at least two days of strength/resistance training.[9]

Now, it's not just about fitting into your favorite jeans or sculpting your muscles. It's about nurturing your cellular health, which is the foundation of your overall well-being. Improved cellular function translates into a reduced risk of chronic diseases, enhanced mental clarity, and sustained energy levels throughout your day.

If you are concerned about finding time or motivation, you're not alone. Life can be hectic, and the couch can be alluring.

---

9   Division of Nutrition, Physical Activity, and Obesity, National Center for Chronic Disease Prevention and Health Promotion, "How Much Physical Activity Do Adults Need?" Centers for Disease Control and Prevention (CDC), last reviewed June 2, 2022, accessed December 15, 2023, www.cdc.gov/physicalactivity/basics/adults/index.htm.

However, there are practical strategies to overcome these obstacles. From squeezing in a quick home workout to finding a workout friend for added motivation, there are ways to make exercise a seamless part of your life.

So, here's the call to action: *Start moving and take the first step toward a healthier, more vibrant you. Your cells are eagerly awaiting the signal to power up. Embrace exercise not just for the mirror's reflection but for the energy, vitality, and well-being that it brings. Your cellular metropolis is ready to thrive, and so are you.*

From Statistic to Success: Transforming Your Health and Vibrancy

According to the latest findings from the CDC, the tragic fact is most adults are missing the mark when it comes to the amount of time they exercise, and this gradually decreases with age.

- In 2020, 28.3% of men and 20.4% of women met the guidelines for both aerobic and muscle-strengthening activities.
- The percentage of men who met both physical activity guidelines decreased with age, from 41.3% of those aged 18–34, to 29.4% of those aged 35–49, to 21.6% of those aged 50–64, and 15.3% of those aged 65 and over.
- The percentage of women who met the guidelines for both physical activities decreased with age, from 28.7% of those aged 18–34, to 22.7% of those aged 35–49, to 17.6% of those aged 50–64, and 10.8% of those aged 65 and over.[10]

---

10 Nazik Elgaddal, MS, Ellen A. Kramarow, PhD, and Cynthia Reuben, MA, "Physical Activity Among Adults Aged 18 and Over: United States, 2020," Centers for Disease Control and Prevention (CDC), August 2022, accessed April 10, 2024, https://www.cdc.gov/nchs/data/databriefs/db443.pdf

EMBRACING MOVEMENT, NO GYM REQUIRED

These statistics are more than just numbers. They are opportunities. Opportunities to take control of our health, to feel better, to live longer, and to embrace vitality.

The journey toward a healthier, more vibrant you begins with a single step, a single choice, a commitment to making movement a part of your life.

You have the power to be among those who break free from the statistics, who defy the odds, and who discover the incredible benefits of regular exercise. It's time to change those numbers. It's time to unlock your potential, to revitalize your cells, and to embrace a life of vibrancy. Are you ready to join the ranks of those who choose health, strength, and vitality?

Imagine a beautiful autumn day, with golden leaves falling gently to the ground. You're young, strolling through the park, reveling in the crisp air and the sense of freedom that comes with it. The world is your oyster, and you feel invincible.

But now, let's fast-forward a few decades. The scene is the same park, the same golden leaves, but something has changed. Your steps are slower, and the simple act of standing up from a park bench feels like a monumental task. Your once-strong legs are no longer as dependable as they used to be.

It's a scenario we all hope to avoid—the loss of independence. You see, the ability to carry bags, rise from a chair, or even manage daily trips to the bathroom independently isn't just about convenience; it's about preserving your vibrancy and freedom.

Let's zoom in on that bathroom scenario for a moment. Imagine having to rely on someone else to help you with this basic, private task. It's not just a physical burden; it's a blow to your dignity and sense of self-reliance. You find yourself yearning for the days when you could effortlessly squat and rise without needing someone to lend a helping hand.

Cardiovascular health and strength are your guardian angels in this story, your keys to preserving independence. It's the power that enables you to easily carry those bags of groceries, lift heavy objects when needed, and, yes, stand up confidently from that chair or toilet. It's the difference between asking for help and confidently saying, "I've got this."

Now, let's rewind to that park bench scenario. Imagine enjoying that crisp autumn day just as you did in your youth. Picture yourself effortlessly rising from the bench, your strong legs carrying you forward with grace. Your vibrant spirit remains untouched, and the world continues to be your oyster.

Finding the Rhythm: A Journey to Vibrant Cardiovascular Health

Cardiovascular exercise, often hailed as the heart-pumping workout, holds the keys to a transformation that goes beyond just physical fitness. It's about infusing your cells with energy, increasing your overall well-being, and embracing life with boundless vitality. Let me share with you the true power of balance in cardio, a lesson I learned when it seemed like time had other plans for my health.

When I first laced up my running shoes and hit the pavement, an exhilarating surge of energy and vitality coursed through me. My heart raced, my breath quickened, and I truly felt on top of the world. But as the miles piled up, something unexpected happened. The very thing that had once invigorated my cells began to take a toll. Running, my love, had become an all-consuming endeavor, draining the very vitality it once sparked. I was in pursuit of a distant horizon, losing sight of the balance my body craved.

Balance, I realized, was the elusive missing piece of the puzzle. It was the key to unlocking the full potential of cardiovascular exercise and vitality. So, on a quest for moderation, I diversified my workouts. I added activities like swimming, cycling, and dancing, and a remarkable transformation took place. The result? An equilibrium that not only elevated my energy levels but also eased the stresses of life and rekindled the vibrancy of my cells.

Finding this balance in your cardio routine is transformative. It can breathe life into your vigor and defy the aging effects that may lurk on the horizon. But it's not about pushing your limits to the edge; it's about crafting a sustainable exercise routine that aligns harmoniously with your body's needs.

Perspective change: Cardiovascular exercise is the heartbeat of your fitness journey, but it's the balance that keeps it steady and robust. So go ahead, embrace the energy, and remember, it's all about finding that perfect rhythm that keeps your cells vibrant and your life in harmony.

Now, let's delve into the world of cardiovascular exercise, often referred to as aerobic or endurance exercise, and learn about its three fundamental principles that you are possibly already aware of:

1. **Elevation in Heart Rate**
2. **Deeper Breaths and Enhanced Oxygen**
3. **Increased Blood Flow and Oxygen to Your Muscles**

Cardiovascular exercise is a cornerstone of any fitness regimen, and here's a fun fact for you: the most prevalent form of cardiovascular exercise might surprise you—it's the simple act of walking!

But that's only one cardio option. Other exhilarating choices include swimming, cycling, hiking, dancing, skating, and, yes, even those passionate moments of intimacy. Regardless of your choice, the key is to engage that heart of yours, get your blood flowing, and unleash the energy within.

You may still be questioning why cardiovascular exercise is so vital. It's not just about elevating your heart rate; it's about sparking life within your cells—the powerhouses of your body. Cardio workouts unlock your body's energy reserves and initiate the production of adenosine triphosphate (ATP), the molecule that fuels your vibrant life.

Not only that, cardiovascular exercise plays a pivotal role in clearing away cellular waste and creating the perfect canvas for fresh, youthful cells to thrive. It's a dynamic process that keeps your body, mind, and cells youthful and thriving.

So, let me ask you: What's your favorite cardio activity? Whether it's a brisk walk, a dance session, a swim, or a passionate run, realize that you're not just exercising; you're laying the foundation for boundless vitality and well-being.

Remember, when you engage in cardiovascular exercise, you're not merely breaking a sweat and boosting your heart rate; you're orchestrating a symphony of vitality within your body. It's a phenomenon where energy is created, waste is expelled, and a fascinating molecule known as nitric oxide (NO) steps into the spotlight.

When your body releases NO during exercise, it's like opening the floodgates for improved circulation, delivering a rush of oxygen and nutrients to every corner of your being.

This miraculous molecule not only enhances blood flow, but it also reduces blood pressure. In fact, NO's discovery led to the creation of the famous little blue pill, Viagra.

Later in this chapter, you will learn about an exercise routine called the Nitric Oxide Dump that takes less than four minutes but offers the physiological benefits of a full thirty minutes of moderate cardiovascular exercise. Time is no longer an excuse for skipping exercise; you can effortlessly fit this routine into your daily life.

No matter your preferred cardiovascular activity, remember that it's more than just a routine—it's your gateway to boundless energy, youthful cells, and a future brimming with vitality.

Strength Training—The Tale of Vibrant Independence

Strength training is a form of physical exercise or workout regimen designed to enhance your muscular strength. It involves the use of resistance, such as weights, resistance bands, or body weight, to challenge and overload the muscles. The goal is to stimulate muscle growth and increase the ability of muscles to generate force. This type of training can lead to improved muscle tone, increased muscle mass, enhanced endurance, and overall physical performance.

Strength training isn't just about building muscles; it's about safeguarding your independence and cherishing your freedom. It's about ensuring that as the years go by, you can still revel in the simple joys of life, like a leisurely stroll in the park on a golden autumn day.

Consider the many aspects of our daily lives that rely on strength, even when we don't realize it. Picture a typical morning. As you rise from bed, you rely on your muscles to support your body weight. As you move through your morning routine, you use strength to lift the kettle, pour a cup of hot coffee, and carry it to the table.

Later, as you head out on errands, you effortlessly pick up your grandchild, cradling them in your arms as they giggle with delight. And when you return home, you confidently carry groceries from the car, knowing that your strength ensures those bags won't weigh you down.

These moments, often taken for granted, are the very essence of everyday strength. Strength training isn't just about achieving impressive feats in the gym; it's about embracing the strength that allows you to navigate life's challenges with ease and grace, ensuring that you can savor each moment to the fullest.

The Battle Against Sarcopenia: Defying the Loss of Muscle Tone

The single most expressed concern among older adults is FALLING and breaking a bone, especially the hip. Yet with the right exercise and movement program, you can eliminate or minimize this fear. But it takes consistent action throughout your lifespan.

As the years pass, our bodies undergo various changes, and one of the most noticeable shifts is the gradual loss of muscle tone. It's a relentless adversary known as sarcopenia, and it affects both men and women. It's like a silent thief, stealthily stealing the strength and vitality that once defined your youth.

Sarcopenia, derived from the Greek words *sarx* (flesh) and *penia* (loss), is more than just a natural consequence of growing older; it's a formidable opponent that can significantly impact your quality of life. Starting around the age of thirty, muscle mass begins to dwindle at a rate of approximately 10 percent per decade. By the time you reach your fifties, this loss accelerates to a staggering 15 percent per decade.[11]

The effects of sarcopenia ripple through every aspect of our daily lives and compromise our independence. Suddenly, tasks that used to be effortless become daunting challenges. Climbing a flight of stairs, carrying groceries, reaching for items on high

---

11 Elena Volpi, Roya Nazemi, and Satoshi Fujita, "Muscle Tissue Changes with Aging," *Current Opinion in Clinical Nutrition and Metabolic Care* 7, no. 4 (2004): 405–10. doi:10.1097/01.mco.0000134362.76653. b2, accessed February 8, 2024, https://pubmed.ncbi.nlm.nih.gov/15192443.

shelves, or even rising from a chair or toilet—all these activities, once taken for granted, can become arduous feats.

The consequences extend beyond physical limitations; sarcopenia can cast a shadow over your overall well-being. Weakening muscles often lead to decreased mobility, making it more challenging to stay active. This, in turn, can result in a sedentary lifestyle, further worsening the issue and setting the stage for a cascade of health problems.

But sarcopenia is not an inevitable fate. Through strength training, you can defy this adversary and regain the muscle strength that time has stolen. Strength training is your defense against sarcopenia, awakening those dormant muscles and breathing life back into them.

When you engage in strength training exercises, you're not merely toning your physique; you're also revitalizing the mitochondria—the cellular powerhouses responsible for converting the food you eat into energy. It's like sending a wake-up call to these vital energy generators, ensuring that they function optimally.

So the next time you lift those weights or engage in resistance training, remember that you're not just sculpting your body; you're defying the march of time. You're taking a stand against sarcopenia, embracing a future where your muscles are still strong, your vitality intact, and your independence preserved. And remember, a little goes a long way; it doesn't have to take massive amounts of time.

As a personal trainer and coach, here are my five practical tips for beginners in strength training:
1. **Start Slowly**, and don't push yourself too hard initially. Begin with exercises that use your body weight as resistance, like squats and push-ups.

2. **Use Proper Form** and techniques to avoid injury. If you're new to more structured exercises, consider working with a trainer or using online resources to learn the right way to perform exercises.
3. **Be Consistent,** and incorporate strength training into your routine at least two to three times a week.
4. **Vary Your Exercises** and workout to target different muscle groups and keep things interesting.
5. **Challenge Yourself** as you progress. Gradually increase the resistance or weight you use. This keeps your muscles engaged and growing.

Remember, it's never too late to start strength training. No matter your age or current fitness level, you can experience the benefits of increased strength, improved metabolism, and a body that defies the effects of aging.

You don't have to be fit to move; you have to move to be fit. Strength training is your path to a vibrant and resilient future.
— Erwan Le Corre, founder of MovNat

The Power of Simple Movement

Have you ever considered that sitting for hours might be silently robbing you of the health, vitality, and freedom you cherish?

Exercise is crucial for building muscular strength and cardiovascular fitness. However, it's essential to remember that even if you engage in regular exercise, spending most of your day in a sedentary position can offset some of those potential benefits. This phenomenon has led to the phrase "sitting is the new smoking," highlighting the importance of continuous movement in our daily lives.

Joan Vernikos, PhD, a NASA researcher specializing in aging and stress, penned the book *Sitting Kills, Moving Heals: How Everyday Movement Will Prevent Pain, Illness, and Early Death—and Exercise Alone Won't*. Drawing on over thirty years of research, she emphasizes that moving every thirty minutes or so is ideal for health span and longevity.[12]

You might be thinking, I can't do that; I have to sit for hours to get my work done. It's a common belief, but if you genuinely desire a healthy and vibrant life, especially after the age of fifty, you need to make room for movement throughout the day, even if it's just for a couple of minutes at a time. Surprisingly, activities like getting up to use the bathroom do indeed count. Even transitioning from sitting to standing alters your heart rate, increases blood flow, and keeps your joints lubricated while engaging your muscles.

Recall the last time you were on a long flight or car ride. How did it feel when you finally stood up and started walking? Your joints probably felt a bit stiff, and it likely took a while to fully regain your mobility. Movement not only helps your body but also sharpens your mind, enhancing your focus and attention.

Maximizing Cellular Health: The Synergy of Movement and Exercise

Movement and exercise are sometimes thought of interchangeably, but they are not the same. To live a vibrant lifestyle, both are critical for cellular health and vitality.

If you're like many people, you may not be aware of all the various movements you do throughout the day. This may include movements such as carrying groceries or packages, climbing stairs,

---

[12] Joan Vernikos, *Sitting Kills, Moving Heals: How Everyday Movement Will Prevent Pain, Illness, and Early Death—and Exercise Alone Won't* (Fresno, CA: Quill Driver Books, 2011).

walking your dog, and reaching for items on the top shelf of your kitchen cabinet. However, exercise tends to result in more strenuous movements and an elevation in your heart rate.

Are you sitting down reading this right now? I would love for you to try the following movements. This is to get you moving while also demonstrating that you can feel more energized in under five minutes.

Revitalize Your Body and Boost Vitality with the Nitric Oxide Dump

Let's get right into it! The Nitric Oxide Dump, created by Zach Bush, MD, is a fantastic four-minute exercise sequence that consists of the following four simple movements that engage all the major muscles in the body.[13]

1. **Squat**—imagine sitting back into a chair and then rising up
2. **Ninety-Degree Arm Swings**—extend your arms in front of you and the movement is up and down
3. **Big Circle**—hands click bottom and top
4. **Straight arms over head/military press**—press hands over your head, as if reaching for the ceiling

Now, here's the challenge: perform these four movements, ten repetitions each, for three sets with your mouth closed (breathing through your nose). Do it three times a day, leaving at least three hours between each workout. If you're like me, you will quickly notice positive changes and even use this when you need to quickly energize your body and mind.

How do you know if you did it right? Once completed, stand still with your arms by your sides. The tingling sensation in your fingertips is the nitric oxide being released, which is a great thing.

---

13 Zach Bush, MD, "ZACH BUSH MD | 4 Minute Workout," YouTube video, 6:36, posted by Zach Bush, MD, May 15, 2017, https://www.youtube.com/watch?v=PwJCJToQmps.

It tells you that your blood is circulating throughout your body. If you feel that, you did it right!

Unlocking Youthful Energy

As kids, we didn't think of play as exercise. It was simply fun. Our youthful days were filled with activities that entertained us, nourished our bodies, and helped us grow healthy and strong from the inside out. The key difference between play and exercise? Perception.

Exercise = Work

Play = Fun!

Back then, the thought of "working out" never crossed our minds. Play was our exercise, and the result? Boundless amounts of energy, the kind that carried us through endless adventures until the sun dipped below the horizon, signaling time for a peaceful night's sleep.

What types of movement activities did you love as a child?

For me, it was hiking in the woods, climbing trees that seemed to touch the sky, riding my bike until the world blurred around me, and diving into a refreshing swimming pool. These weren't just activities; they were expressions of joy, vitality, and the freedom of movement.

But let's face it—aging takes its toll. Our bodies change, and so do our cells. The scientific term for this cellular aging is "senescence." As cells age, they lose their ability to divide and grow, leading to a decline in overall vitality. However, the good news is that there's a powerful antidote to this process: exercise and movement.

So, whether you're young or young at heart, it's time to reclaim the joy of movement and discover the fountain of youth hidden within your cells. Exercise is your ticket to a life filled with boundless energy and the freedom to embrace every moment with enthusiasm and vigor. Let's get ready to unlock your limitless potential for a vibrant, purposeful, and passionate life!

Unlocking Vitality: Harnessing the Power of Exercise for Vibrant Living

Think back for a moment—have you ever experienced a day where you felt tired, lethargic, and stuck in a mental fog? We all have those days. But here's the magic: the very act of moving, of getting up and exercising, can turn that fatigue into boundless energy and clarity.

It's an ironic twist. When you're at your lowest energy ebb and feeling inactive, movement and exercise act as a potent elixir, lifting you up and infusing your being with newfound vitality. As you engage in physical activity, your heart rate quickens, and a rush of oxygen surges into your cells. Then your mitochondria kick into high gear, producing the energy required to chase your dreams and live your best life as a vibrant sage.

But here's the bad news: the longer you lead a sedentary lifestyle, the more your aging cells take the helm. They dominate, and the production of new, vibrant cells dwindles. But here's the incredible news—even if your body has been gripped by sedentary living for years, it's never too late to reignite the fire within. Exercise has the remarkable power to reverse the aging process, breathing new life into your cells and your life. The time to start is now.

Shifting Your Perspective on Exercise: From "Must Do" to "Want to Do"

It's crucial to understand that while weight loss may be a necessary goal for perfecting health and preventing or reversing disease, exercise offers something far more profound: it nurtures the very essence of your well-being, starting at the cellular level. Vibrant health is not just a number on a scale; it's the vitality that radiates from your happy, thriving cells and having the energy you need to live the life you have worked so hard for.

So, whether you've been more of a couch potato or a gym rat, it's critical that you change your perspective on exercise. Here are some things to keep in mind as you begin your transformative journey:

1. Acceptance

Embrace where you are right now without judgment or self-criticism. It's easy to delay starting an exercise program, believing that you need to "get ready" or reach a certain fitness level first. But here's the truth: the best time to start is now. The path to vibrancy begins with accepting your current state, knowing that every step forward is progress.

2. Know Your Why

Take a moment to reflect deeply on your personal motivation. Why does living a vibrant, purposeful, and passionate life matter to you? Think about what drives you, what fuels your desires, and what makes your heart race with excitement. Your "why" can be a powerful source of inspiration. For me, it was a journey toward true health that ignited my purpose—to help others feel amazing as they age.

3. Have Fun

Close your eyes and transport yourself back to your fondest childhood memories of "play." Remember those carefree moments of exploring the woods, kicking a football, or cycling through the neighborhood? Those were times filled with boundless energy and joy. Rediscovering the joy of movement often starts here because it feels less like work and more like play.

4. Schedule Time to Move

Consider when in your day you can dedicate just thirty minutes (or even ten-minute micro-workouts) to movement and exercise. Morning movement and exercise provide a burst of energy, set a positive tone for the day, and minimize distractions.

Midday movement and exercise boost cellular health and enhance focus, making the rest of your day more productive.

Evening movement or exercise doesn't have to be strenuous; a brisk after-dinner walk can be energizing and digestion-enhancing, suitable for all.

5. Embrace Action

Now that you've figured out your exercise schedule, it's time to act and plan your exercise/play sessions. This step can be challenging, especially if it's been a while since you've been active or if exercise doesn't naturally bring you joy. But remember, exercise is not merely a "must-do" chore; it's your gateway to a more vibrant life. Every step, no matter how small, is a step closer to a life filled with vitality, purpose, and passion.

So, lace up those sneakers, grab your workout gear, and get moving. Your path to vibrancy begins right here, right now.

Embracing Exercise with Enthusiasm

Now that you understand exercise's pivotal role in leading a vibrant and purposeful life, let's dive into the "how." If the idea of exercise hasn't thrilled you in the past, fear not! Here are nine suggestions to help you not only embrace exercise but also find joy on your path to a healthier and more vibrant you:

1. Turn Play into Exercise

Why not make exercise feel like playtime? Whether it's walking your dog, sharing a brisk stroll with a friend, or indulging in lively activities with your grandkids, find an activity that gets your heart racing and brings joy to your day.

2. Build Functional Strength

Incorporate regular strength and resistance training into your routine. It's not just about lifting weights; it's about building resilience and functional strength that enhances your everyday life.

3. Stay Active throughout the Day

Set reminders to move every thirty minutes. These short, frequent breaks will do wonders for your cellular health and overall well-being.

4. Make It a Social Experience

Exercise becomes more enjoyable when shared. Consider joining a gym, a community center, or simply inviting a friend to join you on your fitness journey.

5. Rediscover Old Sports

Dust off your old sports equipment and relive those active moments. Whether it's tennis, golf, or basketball, enjoy the nostalgia while staying active and safe.

6. Elevate Your Heart Rate

Engage in heart-pumping exercises, such as brisk walking, to invigorate your body and mind.

7. Find an Exercise Buddy

Having someone by your side, whether it's a friend or a personal trainer, can provide motivation, guidance, and safety as you pursue a healthier lifestyle.

8. Integrate Movement Naturally

Make movement a seamless part of your daily routine. Take a walk before or after meals, stretch in the morning, or indulge in a playful activity like a pillow fight or tag game for added fun.

9. Prioritize Joy and Recreation

I'm repeating this because it's so vital. Engage in activities that bring joy and recreation into your life, whether it's hiking, biking, dancing, or any other activity that makes your heart sing.

The key to a vibrant life lies in making exercise an enjoyable part of your daily routine. Embrace these suggestions, and you'll find yourself looking forward to each opportunity to move and invigorate your body and mind.

Your Stories, Beliefs, and Dreams Inspire Your Actions!

> *It is often the smaller pleasures in life that have the greatest impact on one's happiness.*
> — EPICURUS

Now, let's get into the heart of movement, where stories of transformation come alive. I'll share two remarkable stories that demonstrate the power of embracing movement as a key to vibrant aging. These are more than anecdotes; they are proof that it's never too late to harness the energy, vitality, and joy that movement can bring.

So, immerse yourself in these stories and feel the passion, the struggle, and the triumphs. Let them reaffirm the boundless potential within you on your journey to becoming a vibrant sage. We'll start with one captivating story, followed by interviews with a client who has experienced this transformation firsthand and a professional who has dedicated her career to helping others discover the beauty of movement. Together, these narratives will illuminate the path forward.

Rediscovering Vitality: Fred's Journey from Retirement to Active Living

Once a college athlete with a penchant for an active life, Fred, in his early seventies, found himself navigating the uncharted waters of retirement. As the rhythm of his days slowed, his body seemed to respond in kind, settling into a more sedentary existence. Fred had become slow, easily fatigued, and often struggled to rise from the floor, an essential skill when surrounded by young, energetic grandchildren.

However, his wife, a spirited partner of over four decades and eight years his junior, envisioned travel, community engagements, and treasured moments spent with their grandchildren. She yearned for those golden years to be as vibrant as the rest of their life together had been, for them to walk the world's paths hand in hand, and for Fred to have the stamina to keep up.

Her plea to me was direct: "You have to do something with my husband." And so I listened, her words echoing with a deep love for the man who had shared her adventures, her dreams, and her life. She conveyed her frustrations, her concern that the adventures they cherished were slipping away.

So, with a shared dream and a loving nudge from his wife, Fred and I started working together. He was friendly, cooperative, and undeniably motivated, not just because it was what his wife wished for, but because he too had dreams and plans that involved vitality and strength.

His program began with a comprehensive evaluation, and together we charted a course toward rejuvenation. Thirty minutes, twice a week, became our compass, and Fred was a stalwart companion on this path to renewal. There was no room for nonsense; we were here for a purpose.

It didn't take long—only two months—before we started to see the remarkable changes. But it was one particular story Fred shared with me that truly encapsulated his journey, his pride shining through. It demonstrated that his transformation was not merely physical; it was a story of empowerment, resilience, and the enduring spirit that refuses to accept limitations.

It was a Monday morning, about eight weeks into training. Fred came into the session beaming with pride; the room seemed to brighten with his excitement. He shared that over the weekend, his granddaughter, who weighed almost thirty pounds, had been visiting and, at one point, was perched on his lap. Without a second thought, he stood up effortlessly and carried her with him.

I looked at him and said, "Wow, that's amazing!"

That's when he realized I hadn't grasped the full significance of the story and continued talking.

"Two months ago, I would have taken her off my lap and placed her next to me so that I could then push myself out of the chair. After that, I would have picked her up. This time I just STOOD UP!"

Fred's achievement wasn't just about lifting his granddaughter; it was about lifting the weight of limitations and welcoming new possibilities. His journey, like many others, began with a specific fitness goal but blossomed into something far more profound, empowering him to lead a fuller, more vibrant life.

I was so proud of him! His determination and dedication to improving not just his fitness level but also his life, both for himself and his family, were incredible.

Now, take a moment to reflect. How has exercise changed your life, or where could improved strength, balance, endurance, and flexibility make a difference? Stretch your mind to new dimensions and add some imagination to your answer.

If you do NOT exercise, which area(s) of your life could be enriched if you began to include cardio, strength, balance, endurance, and flexibility training? Stretch your mind to new dimensions and add some imagination for this answer.

Minerva's Journey: From Strength Training to World Travel

Meet Minerva, a woman of remarkable vision and zest for life. Several years before her retirement, she began working out to build strength and stamina, fueled by the dream of exploring the world on her terms. As she approached her golden years, her determination and commitment to vibrant aging fueled her transformation.

In the spring of 2019, I had the privilege of reuniting with Minerva. Our paths had crossed a few years prior, and during those encounters, she would often remark, "I really need to exercise, but I'm so busy." But now, it seemed that the stars had finally aligned, and this was the perfect time for Minerva to act. She had two upcoming trips, and she knew that if she wanted to have the best experience, she needed to enhance her stamina, strength, and balance.

Minerva, in her early sixties, held two profound desires close to her heart that ignited the flames of her transformation. First and foremost was her deep connection with her family. She yearned to play an active role in her children's and future grandchildren's lives for years to come. And second was her desire to travel. Her eyes sparkled with anticipation as she spoke of the grand adventures awaiting her and her husband—trips to the enchanting island of Hawaii and the romantic cobblestone streets of Italy.

Beneath Minerva's seemingly boundless determination lay the pressures of a demanding career. Hours of sitting and the weight of stress had taken their toll. She realized that if she wanted to retire with the best health and vitality she craved, she couldn't afford to wait any longer.

Minerva had always been on the move, enjoying activities like walking and cycling as part of her daily life. While she was far from being sedentary, structured exercise had never been a priority.

With Minerva's demanding work schedule in mind, I crafted a hybrid training program that blended in-person and virtual sessions. This program focused on improving her balance, coordination, endurance, and strength—elements that were key to her future adventures.

Minerva committed to training three days a week, often with her husband by her side. Within just three weeks, the improvements in her balance, strength, and coordination were already clear. We were both thrilled to see her progress, which served as a powerful motivator for her to continue her fitness journey.

But why was balance so crucial? It's simple—many individuals fear falling as they age. And often, the fear of falling itself increases the likelihood of it happening. This fear can lead to avoiding activities that demand balance, like climbing mountains or navigating rocky terrain. Avoiding these cherished activities is no way to live vibrantly.

After a mere three months of dedicated training, Minerva confidently announced she was no longer fearful of falling. A few weeks later, she went on her Italian adventure, and her message to me resonated with newfound vibrancy: "I felt boundless energy coursing through me as I gracefully wandered the cobblestone streets of Rome!" Her joy radiated both from within and without.

Minerva's journey proves that it's never too late to make a change and pursue the life you desire, both in the present and the future. Her story is a testament to the enduring power of movement and the pursuit of vibrant well-being.

Catching Up with Minerva: A 2023 Update

In 2019, Minerva set out on a life-changing path toward a vibrant retirement, welcoming fitness and well-being with unwavering determination. In early 2023, I caught up with Minerva to see how her vibrant journey has continued to shape her life and well-being.

Retired!

In September 2022, Minerva and her husband began their shared retirement adventure. Minerva had planned to retire at the end of the year but decided not to wait any longer due to the stress of her job. Together, they had prepared for a fulfilling retirement, and Minerva realized there was no reason to delay her well-deserved freedom.

Minerva's three months of intensive personal training and coaching in 2019 had laid the foundation for her vibrant retirement. She had learned how to build strength, maintain balance, and exercise safely. She embraced a holistic approach to fitness and understood that it was not only about physical strength but also about discipline, stamina, and balance.

One of the most significant transformations she shared was in her balance. Initially struggling to stand on one leg for even a few seconds, she diligently practiced and improved over time. This improved balance not only enhanced her daily life but also instilled confidence as she ventured onto uncertain terrains during her travels.

In retirement, Minerva brought her fitness qualities to the forefront. Stamina, strength, and discipline became her allies as she explored new destinations. Long walks and challenging hikes became part of her daily routine, while discipline helped her maintain a healthy diet and consistent exercise routine, even during cruises filled with tempting culinary offerings.

Her daily exercise routine was nonnegotiable, whether she was at home or off exploring the world. In retirement, where she and her husband enjoyed traveling, stamina was a valuable asset. They explored different countries, immersed themselves in excursions, and created memories without the limitations of fatigue or physical weakness.

Technology played a role in Minerva's motivation, with her sons gifting her an Apple Watch. Seeing the rings close after each workout became a satisfying ritual, encouraging her to stay active and support her health.

With her vibrant retirement in full swing, Minerva had sage advice for those nearing or in retirement: "It's your time to enjoy life to the fullest. Relax, take care of yourself, and minimize stress whenever possible. Nurture your body and mind, and don't forget to plan for the future, no matter your age."

Her life was a testament to the power of planning; Minerva had kept five-year plans since her twenties, helping her remain focused on her goals and dreams. Even in retirement, she had a plan—cruising the world with her husband for the next couple of years, followed by cherishing moments with her future grandchildren.

Could a vibrant retirement, filled with exciting adventures and boundless energy, be within your reach, regardless of your age? Minerva's journey suggests that the path to vibrant aging is open to those willing to take the first step. What might your path look like?

Letting Go of the Ego for Vibrant Well-Being

Back in my teenage years, I was as flexible as a rubber band, effortlessly doing splits without breaking a sweat. However, fast-forward two decades to the mid-1990s, and it felt like my flexibility had vanished into thin air. This realization prompted me to explore yoga as a means of regaining my lost flexibility.

I took my first yoga class at a local YMCA when I was around thirty-five years old. The instructor was a remarkable woman in her midsixties. She shared with us her incredible journey: a decade ago, she had been diagnosed with rheumatoid arthritis and had been told that she'd eventually be in a wheelchair. In response, she immersed herself in the practice of yoga, and here she was, teaching yoga and bending in ways I could only dream of (even in my cheerleading days, which suddenly felt like a distant memory).

The class was challenging, and it wasn't the postures or poses that troubled me; it was my own ego. I couldn't fathom how I struggled to keep up with a sixty-plus-year-old woman. The embarrassment lingered, and it would be another fifteen years before I dared step into another yoga class.

Have you ever felt so intimidated by someone's abilities that it held you back from pursuing an activity you were genuinely interested in?

Fast-forward a decade, and my yoga practice remained inconsistent. I'd be enthusiastic to start, but then I'd be unable to commit for more than a few months at a time, largely due to my inflexibility and ego issues.

However, my breathwork training with Michaël B. opened my eyes to the profound scope of yoga. I realized that yoga was not just about flexibility; it encompassed a vast realm of holistic well-being. Even though I was still far from being a contortionist, I made a resolute decision not just to be a yoga practitioner but to undertake a two-hundred-hour yoga training.

In my quest to find the ideal instructor, I stumbled upon Cathy Madeo, an extraordinary yoga teacher with an impressive presence on social media. Every post was inspiring yet intimidating, making me wonder how she performed such incredible feats. The more I learned about her, the more intrigued I became about her yoga teacher training program and whether it was right for me. During our conversation, she assured me that flexibility wasn't a prerequisite for the course. That was the moment I decided to take the leap and enroll.

Conversation with Cathy Madeo—Embracing Yoga, Healing, and Fitness

Cathy Madeo is so much more than an extraordinary yoga teacher and a beautiful, compassionate person. She is a fighter!

In this exclusive interview, I explore her unique approach to yoga, her painful yet inspiring journey, her tenacity to never give up, and the valuable insights she offers for those looking to lead vibrant lives. Through this conversation, you'll gain valuable wisdom and discover that age is no barrier to achieving your dreams, finding inner balance, and embracing a holistic approach to well-being.

As you read this interview, I encourage you to take a moment to reflect on your own experiences, challenges, and any self-doubts that may have impeded your fitness goals. Allow her story and wisdom to ignite your fitness journey.

Q: Please share a bit about your journey that led you to where you are today. While you're a yoga instructor, I assume your path involves more than just yoga. Can you give us a brief overview?

I started my journey actually as a young tennis player. My whole family was into tennis. We lived in a small town in West Virginia. At the age of ten, we moved to Florida, which is like the mecca of training tennis players. And during the summer, I would do tennis camps, and then I started to do sanctioned tournaments, which is like amateur pro stuff. I was nationally ranked. Yet at the age of sixteen, I left tennis, but what I developed as a serious, hard-working tennis player was discipline. When a lot of people say to me now, "Oh, you're so prolific with everything you do, you do so much, you're so disciplined," I actually attribute it to that time.

Q: How did you discover yoga?

I was nineteen and attending a theater conservatory in Chicago to be an actor. Each semester, as part of the training, we had a movement focus. This was a long time ago, around 1994, almost thirty years ago. One of the semesters, the movement focus was yoga. Back then, there weren't a whole lot of yoga studios. The class was at this man's apartment, he was an Iyengar instructor. We showed up to his apartment for the first time, and he's got dreadlocks, no shirt on, tiny black shorts. We had to sit in these postures for what felt like twenty, thirty minutes—I'm sure it was only a few minutes. Next, he would actually talk about yoga philosophy. And I had grown up very spiritual when I was young, and I had found all these meditation books. And so hearing him talk and then having a physical part, I was like, I have found what I have been searching for since the age of sixteen.

Q: So you have been practicing yoga since you were nineteen?

Yes. Shortly after that semester in Chicago, I moved to Los Angeles to pursue acting. It was also considered the mecca of yoga, so as soon as I got there, I found a yoga studio. For the next ten years, throughout my twenties, I practiced yoga before I did any teacher training.

Q: As you pursued yoga, were you doing other forms of movement, exercise?

I was always active. In LA, I would go hiking or for a run. I am a mover. You know, I love that you used the word movement. When I'm not taking a yoga class, I'm moving my body somehow. I'm one of those people who if you ask me what I want to do, I will suggest something active, like standup paddleboard or going for a walk on the beach.

Q: How has your yoga practice evolved?

There was a period of five to ten years where I almost got a little bit of ego or pride around that where I was just practicing yoga. I believed that I'm just going to do yoga. I have these strong muscles, and I don't need cardio because everyone says you do. I decided that I was going to show the world that you don't, you know, all this stuff. Then I went through my spine stuff. I had a history of spine injury, and that changed everything for me. I really learned that while yoga is an excellent discipline of movement, it's not everything.

Q: Please share your spinal injury story and recovery. The pain you must have experienced is something I hope my readers will never endure. When you shared your story, I couldn't help but think, How in the world did she do that? Watching you today, no one would have any idea. But what is most amazing is that what you experienced could have resulted in you never practicing yoga ever again and living a life of chronic pain. It just amazes me because so many of us have sustained an injury that has derailed us from engaging in not only activities we love but also has an impact on our mental well-being. Can you share a little bit and also some insight?

It is an important topic. You're a human being. At some point, you're going to experience a physical injury to some degree. And you're right, it can kind of make us or break us. And so in some ways, our recovery has a lot to do with our mindset, you know, and what we believe to be true. I was born with a spinal condition. And while the movement and the yoga weren't the reason I needed surgery, I recognized what I had done before was not going to help me move forward. My surgery did not go well, and I was in a very dark place in my healing process. It was a really tough and long recovery. I didn't even think of it so much as an age thing because I was in such a dark place, and my body was in so much pain that I didn't even know what I needed to do. But I realized that it's definitely hard to do things differently because it was what I had done before that got me to where I was.

Q: How did you get out of what you refer to as a "very dark place"?

The pain was unbearable for a long time—there was a point I refer to as an apex, the climax of really intense pain. I allowed myself to go into this dark, alienating place. I think that anyone who goes through chronic pain understands, but others simply cannot understand the darkness that comes from chronic pain. Healing is a very personal process. And so it suddenly became very clear to me, Nancy, that I wasn't going to get healed by anyone outside of me. Like this was going to be me that had to heal, you know? And I was going to need to figure this out.

I approached healing and movement differently. A switch went off in my mind that I had to be very gentle with my body. Truly not forcing things. Movement became gentle, such as simply rotating my hands and warming up my wrist joint—stretching my chest was movement and moving energy. I had to reconnect with my body and learn how it moves and feels—recognizing the sensations in my body. I had to recognize the difference between pain versus discomfort.

Q: Could you explain what you mean by pain versus discomfort?

When I would move and do gentle movements as I was healing, I was getting more clarity on what was pain versus discomfort. This was important for me. I believe that for many of us, after an injury, we become scared of making the injury worse, and we make things worse by not doing anything. This happens because when we are not moving, our body gets stiff, tight, and weak. Once I was able to understand discomfort and be in certain postures that didn't feel comfortable but weren't painful, everything changed. It took about one year to recover.

Q: Wow, I had no idea that your recovery was such a difficult, painstaking process involving such small, minute steps. When I watch you perform different postures and movements, I am in awe.

You have no idea. I really did begin with simply moving my wrist and taking deep breaths to feel my chest expand and get energy flowing throughout my body. It was a challenge. During my journey back, I took things easy, simple, one step at a time. For example, planks were performed against the wall. Now I can't do any backbends, and I have a lot of limited mobility, but the other part of me is like, it is incredible. I'm more flexible than I've ever been in my life, and I'm forty-nine years old. Since my surgery, and with my self-recovery, I believe I am my strongest and most flexible now.

Q: Yoga can be intimidating for someone who doesn't practice. What are some yoga myths?

It is important to know that there are many types of yoga styles, making it accessible to everyone. One common myth is that yoga is simply gentle stretching, or it is not challenging. There are many styles of yoga and a range as it relates to levels of challenge. For example, a power yoga class will be very different and more intense than a Yin yoga class. Both are excellent styles but different, and yes, some can be very challenging, like power yoga, while others are gentler, like Yin, restorative, or senior yoga.

Another common myth pertains to flexibility. Flexibility is not a requirement at all to either take part in or gain benefits from a yoga class. There are so many different forms of yoga—there is something for everyone. What is important when you first start taking yoga classes is to do research ahead of time. Check out the studio's website, class descriptions, and the owner's background. If you are still not sure, call the studio and ask questions.

Lastly, while most of the formats do require movement on and off the floor, not all do. Chair yoga has gained tremendous popularity in recent years to help solve this problem. This also reflects how yoga is for everyone. This isn't just for seniors. Many adults have sustained injuries or may have neuromuscular disorders that prevent them from accessing a traditional class. But with chair yoga, you get all the benefits without the fear. There is also gentle and restorative yoga.

Q: Where should a person new to movement start?

Baby steps are always a great approach to anything. Small, short, consecutive movements accumulated over a long period of time give you the best results. I actually attribute a lot of my fitness and regaining my health and youthfulness to just that. I don't spend hours at the gym. I'm not working out three, four hours a day. I do these short little bursts of time. But I do them every day. And that, accumulated over the decades that I've been doing this, has given me a fit, capable body, right? And so you don't need to do a lot, but you do need to be consistent. Start with ten minutes a day. If you're not doing anything and you suddenly just commit to ten minutes a day, okay, I'm going to walk and do some gentle stretching. Gradually start to walk a little longer than ten minutes.

Q: Thank you, Cathy, for your insights.

Cathy's journey and insights are a testament to the power of resilience and adaptability. Her story highlights that age, injuries, or limitations need not hinder our pursuit of well-being. Before moving on to the next pillar, let's review these valuable insights and reflect on how they can be applied to our own lives as we strive to become vibrant sages.

Discipline as a Foundation

Cathy's discipline, cultivated during her tennis years, became a cornerstone of her success in various aspects of life. It's a reminder that discipline can be a powerful tool for achieving our goals, regardless of our age.

Embrace Change

Cathy's transition from tennis to acting and later to yoga shows the importance of being open to change and exploring new avenues for personal growth.

Yoga as a Lifelong Practice

Cathy's enduring yoga practice, spanning three decades, emphasizes that yoga is accessible to everyone, regardless of age or flexibility. It's not about contorting your body into challenging poses; it's about finding what works for you and honoring your body's needs.

Overcome Challenges

Cathy's story of spinal surgery and her journey from darkness to empowerment showcases the resilience of the human spirit. Her approach to healing and rediscovering her body's capabilities offers hope and inspiration to anyone facing physical challenges or chronic pain.

Consistency and Small Steps

Cathy's fitness philosophy underscores that consistent, small, and manageable steps can lead to remarkable results over time. It's a reminder that you don't need to commit hours to exercise daily; consistency and gradual progress can make a significant impact.

As you reflect on Cathy's journey and insights, consider how her experiences align with your aspirations for a vibrant life. Her story invites us to welcome discipline, adapt to change, and celebrate self-discovery through movement and mindfulness.

Please see the Acknowledgments and Contact Information section at the end of the book for more details about Cathy Madeo.

Vibrant Living: Movement, Play, and Inspirational Tales

As you strive to live your most vibrant life, let's take a moment to draw inspiration from these three remarkable individuals who discovered the transformative power of exercise at various stages of life.

First Fred, a loving grandfather in his seventies. For him, exercise isn't just about staying fit; it's about preserving his independence. Fred understands that strength and mobility are his tickets to enjoying quality time with his grandchildren, whether it's a game of tag in the backyard or chasing them down the park's winding paths. He embodies the belief that age should never be a barrier to experiencing life's joys to the fullest.

Then there's Minerva, a retiree with a heart full of dreams. In her newfound freedom, Minerva has embarked on adventures she'd only dreamed of during her working years. From hiking scenic trails to dancing the night away with friends, Minerva's retirement is a vibrant tapestry of experiences. She attributes her boundless energy and enthusiasm to her commitment to regular exercise, which not only keeps her fit but also fuels her zest for life.

And last but certainly not least, there's Cathy—a testament to the incredible potential for transformation. Cathy, a lifelong athlete who, at the age of forty, sustained a spinal injury that almost yielded life in a wheelchair and chronic excruciating pain most of us could not imagine. However, she took the first step toward change, embracing simple movements that gradually transformed her life. Her inspiring story reminds us that it is important to listen to our body, that it's never too late to regain our health, well-being, and fitness.

Through Cathy, Minerva, and Fred, we discover that vitality is waiting within each of us.

With each step, each heart-pounding moment, and each joyful game, these individuals aren't just exercising and moving; they're igniting the spark of life within them. They're nurturing their cells, their bodies, and their spirits.

As we close this chapter on the second pillar of vibrant aging, remember that exercise is one of your greatest allies in the pursuit of a vibrant life. Whether you're starting from a place of injury and pain like Cathy, looking to welcome retirement with the enthusiasm of Minerva, or cherishing your independence like Fred, you're one step closer to the vibrant, purposeful, and passionate life you deserve.

As we embark on our journey through Pillar Three, nutrition, get ready to uncover the profound impact that food has on our bodies. Just as with breath and movement, nutrition plays a pivotal role in shaping our vibrant lives. So join me in exploring how the choices we make in the kitchen can lead to greater vitality and a life filled with purpose and passion.

*Take a moment to reflect on this question:
What inspires you to embrace exercise and movement as vital
allies on your path to a purposeful and passionate life?*

CHAPTER 6

PILLAR THREE

EVOLVING NUTRITION... IT'S NOT ABOUT THE CALORIES

*Good nutrition creates health in all areas of our existence.
All parts are interconnected.*
— T. Colin Campbell

So far, we've seen how breath and movement form the foundation of our vibrant journey; now let's add the nutritional component. Nutrition is more than just fuel—it's the very essence of our health and has a profound impact on our overall well-being.

Take a moment to assess your relationship with nutrition. What does nutrition mean to you? How have the foods you've consumed shaped your health and overall well-being? Have you ever been on a diet, and if so, how did it affect you?

For much of my life, I gave little thought to the intricate dance between food and well-being. Calories and weight were at the forefront, while the true power of nutrients and their impact on health remained hidden beneath the surface. In this chapter, join me on a personal journey that transformed my perspective from a focus on calories and a rigid lifestyle to a profound understanding of how the foods we eat can profoundly shape our health and our lives.

A Journey to Understanding Health: Navigating Influences and Choices

Throughout most of my life, I considered myself a healthy eater. Sweets were never a great temptation, and my penchant for cooking with whole, unprocessed foods kept me on a seemingly virtuous path. It wasn't until mid-2010 that I embraced a specific type of lifestyle diet—I decided to follow a vegetarian lifestyle. Sometimes I wonder why I chose this way of eating, but the answer remains elusive. Perhaps it was the influence of friends, an article I read, or maybe it was a personal challenge I set for myself. Regardless, I distinctly recall being at the airport in New York, about to board a flight to a conference in San Jose, California. It was in that moment that I made a seemingly impulsive decision: no more meat. Maybe it was because all the airport food options seemed to revolve around processed meats; I can't say for sure. For the next year, I wholeheartedly embraced a vegetarian lifestyle, convinced it was a responsible and health-conscious choice. My plate overflowed with vibrant fruits, hearty legumes, crunchy veggies, and protein-rich tofu. However, fast-forward a year, and my vitality took an unexpected nosedive. I wasn't just tired—I was utterly exhausted. My mind felt perpetually foggy, and during a half-marathon, one side of my body briefly went numb. Have you ever made a dietary choice that seemed right at the time, only to question it later?

A visit to my doctor was my next step. I had blood tests done, and the conclusion? Alarmingly low iron levels. What followed was a medical whirlwind—oncologists, gastroenterologists, and even a colonoscopy. The big medical words all boiled down to one term: anemia of unknown origin. The prescription? An iron pill and a reluctant bite of a hamburger after a yearlong hiatus.

Taking that first savory bite of meat was a revelation for me. Over time, with the combination of beef and iron supplements, my health stabilized. My takeaway? It wasn't about the universal merits of any specific diet—it was about recognizing and honoring what my body needed. While some thrive on plant-based diets, my experience underscored the importance of tuning in and listening to my body's signals.

In 2013, whispers of the Paleo diet reached my ears, painting a tantalizing picture of ancient culinary simplicity. I found myself stepping on the scale and watching in disbelief as the numbers dropped—a full ten pounds lighter. Was it the sweat from my workouts or the new menu on my plate? I could only guess.

Feeling light and jubilant, I credited most of my transformation to my new diet. But there was a blind spot. I was so engrossed, so singularly focused on chasing the silhouette of my younger self, that I missed three unmistakable signals that all was not well:

1. The afternoon fatigue that clung to me like a persistent shadow.
2. The nighttime cramps that turned bedtime into a nightly battle.
3. The dense fog in my brain; a shroud that slowed my every thought at work.

Each time a friend or colleague would tilt their head, eyes filled with concern, and ask, "Are you okay?" a tiny crack formed in my confidence. Was this radiant image I saw in the mirror just an illusion?

In the race to recapture the energy and physique of my youth, I had to ask myself, Had I forgotten to listen to the whispers of my body, telling me it needed more?

Transitioning from Diet to Lifestyle

It's fairly common to be influenced by popular diets or external pressures that prompt us to alter our eating habits. Motivations for these changes may include weight loss goals, health concerns, or simply the desire to try something new. We've all heard of diets like keto, veganism, South Beach, and various plans that exclude fats, sugars, or salt. These dietary trends can be intriguing, promising quick results and a path to improved well-being.

During our younger years, experimenting with different diets may seem harmless and, occasionally, even beneficial. However, as we mature, it becomes increasingly crucial to attune ourselves to our body's ever-changing needs. While some diets may deliver temporary results, they often don't live up to their promises.

It's essential to recognize that a truly effective and beneficial dietary choice isn't just a passing phase. When a way of eating aligns seamlessly with our body's requirements, consistently making us feel invigorated and healthy, it transcends the label of a diet. It becomes a way of life.

But it's important to exercise caution before jumping into the latest dietary trend. Instead, prioritize understanding and listening to your body. The human body often has an innate wisdom that can guide us toward the nutrients it requires, especially as we age. All we need to do is pay attention.

Have you ever been swayed by a dietary trend, only to later question its long-term impact on your well-being? Many of us have. Your food choices matter more than you may realize. It's not just about counting calories; it's about nourishing your body with the right nutrients, the ones that get absorbed into your cells, fueling your energy, and supporting your overall well-being. If you're grappling with chronic health conditions, persistently low energy levels, or a compromised immune system, now might be the perfect time to take a closer look at your nutrition.

So let's delve deeper into the intricacies of nutrition and learn how the foods you choose can nourish your body as well as your soul to create a more vibrant and passionate life. You'll discover that you can tap into your inner wisdom to make choices that make you feel better and also support your inner sage.

Unveiling the Wisdom of Nutrition

We have a great opportunity to get on the right side of this battle by beginning to think differently about the way that we eat and the way that we approach food.

— Marcus Samuelsson

The science of nutrition is complex and confusing. Food is much more than fuel, and figuring out the best foods to eat, when to eat, and other variables to perfect an individual's health can be a huge challenge.

Navigating the world of nutrition can be quite a puzzle for several reasons: The media and the internet bombard us with vast and often contradictory information about food and diets. Yet our bodies are unique, and how our cells and organs process and use micro- and macronutrients can vary greatly from person to person. Furthermore, our nutritional needs evolve throughout our lives due to the changing demands of our bodies.

Now, let's tackle a fundamental question: How do we truly extract the nutritional goodness from the food we eat? At first glance, the answer seems straightforward—just eat it. But it's a bit more intricate than that.

The intricate nature of nutrition breaks down into three key areas:

1. Digestion
2. Gut Biome
3. Genomics/DNA

Unlocking the Secrets of Digestion

Imagine a day when you woke up feeling on top of the world. You had a spring in your step, a clear mind, and boundless energy. It was going to be a fantastic day.

But as the day progressed, you noticed something happening in your body. A subtle discomfort began to creep in. Maybe it was a gassy sensation that refused to subside or a persistent stomachache that lingered like an unwelcome guest.

As the discomfort grew, you realized it was taking over your thoughts. You found it challenging to focus on your tasks, conversations, or anything at all. Your enthusiasm for the day was replaced by a sense of malaise.

That feeling of being on top of the world had vanished, and you couldn't help but wonder what had gone wrong.

You see, your digestive system is like the control center of your body. When it's running smoothly, you hardly notice it. But when things go awry, it can turn your day upside down.

The discomfort in your gut wasn't just physical; it had a ripple effect on your entire well-being. It was as if your body's harmony had been disrupted, and you were knocked out of sync.

In that moment, you realized the truth: your digestive system plays a pivotal role in how you feel and function each day. When it's not working as it should, it's challenging to be at your best. That's the power it holds over your overall well-being.

Though digestion might not be the most glamorous topic, it's an unsung hero of your health and vibrancy. Every bite you take, every morsel you savor, undergoes a remarkable transformation within your body.

From the moment food touches your lips, a symphony of processes kicks into gear. Digestion isn't just about breaking down what you eat; it's about extracting the vital nutrients that your body craves for optimal functioning.

In the realm of nutrients, we have two classes: macronutrients and micronutrients. The former, also known as "macros," are proteins, carbohydrates, and fats that provide your body with the necessary energy to fuel your daily life. The latter, micronutrients, are vitamins and minerals. These are needed in smaller amounts but play crucial roles in warding off diseases and supporting health and overall well-being.

Now, consider this: digestion doesn't just begin when you take your first bite. It starts even before food enters your mouth. That delightful aroma of a freshly baked pie or a savory stir-fry? It triggers your salivary glands, and as your mouth waters, digestion is already underway.

The digestion process consists of four stages.

First, the Mouth. Here, your food meets the first wave of digestive enzymes, courtesy of your saliva. Chewing further dissects the morsels, breaking them into smaller, more manageable pieces. The journey continues as you swallow, sending the food on its way to the stomach.

Then, the Stomach. Upon reaching the stomach, your meal faces a harsher environment. Powerful acids and enzymes launch a second assault on your food, breaking it down further. The stomach also serves as a temporary storage facility before ushering its contents into the small intestine.

Next, the Small Intestine. The small intestine, a remarkable organ, continues the digestive process. Enzymes here further break down your meal into its constituent parts. This is where the magic happens—most of the essential nutrients are absorbed through the walls of the small intestine, ready to fuel your body.

Finally, the Large Intestine. The remnants of your meal reach the large intestine, also known as the colon. Here, any undigested food and waste products undergo final processing before being eliminated from your body as stool.

Have you ever wondered just how long this incredible journey from your plate to your rear end takes? According to the Mayo Clinic, on average, it's a mere thirty-six hours from the moment your fork meets food to the final exit through the mysterious realm of your anus.[14] It's a marvel of nature, a captivating testament to the intricate yet seamlessly automatic processes your body orchestrates to nourish and sustain you.

The Power of Your Gut Microbiome: Your Body's Thriving Community

Your gut is a vibrant city within your body, bustling with trillions of microorganisms. These microscopic residents form what we call the gut microbiome, a dynamic community that plays a crucial role in nearly every aspect of our well-being—from sleep quality to immune strength, mood, and overall performance.

In a world where we often associate bacteria and viruses with illness, it might surprise you to learn that this bustling city of microorganisms is essential to your health. Your gut microbiome

---

[14] Elizabeth Rajan, MD, "Digestion: How Long Does It Take?" Mayo Clinic, accessed February 8, 2024, https://www.mayoclinic.org/digestive-system/expert-answers/faq.

consists of trillions of bacteria, viruses, fungi, and their genetic material, all living in both your small and large intestines.

What's fascinating is that your gut microbiome is as unique as you are. It's initially shaped by your DNA and then influenced by a myriad of factors, including your environment, medications, genetics, and even psychological factors like stress.

However, supporting a harmonious balance in this bustling metropolis of microorganisms is no easy task. Just think about how you feel when your stomach is upset or you're dealing with gas—it can be downright miserable, far from the vibrancy we all desire.

So, what does your digestive system need? To function optimally, it requires a harmonious blend of these diverse microorganisms—thousands of different species all working together. A healthy gut is essential for the efficient absorption of nutrients. Even if you're consuming nutrient-rich foods, an unhealthy gut can impede the absorption of essential vitamins and minerals, leaving your cells without the nourishment they need to thrive.

The Power of Your DNA and Epigenetics

In addition to digestion and the gut microbiome, your DNA has a significant influence on your body's ability to absorb and use the information from the various vitamins and nutrients.

In the earlier chapters, we explored the intricate world of DNA and epigenetics and how these factors intertwine with our lifestyle, habits, and behaviors. As we've learned, DNA and epigenetics leave their fingerprints on every facet of our existence, shaping who we are at our core. Yet, there's one realm where their influence shines especially bright, and that's the world of nutrition.

Just like a skilled chef relies on the right ingredients and techniques to create a masterpiece in the kitchen, your DNA and epigenetics supply the ultimate recipe for your health and vitality. They decide how your body responds to the nutrients you provide it, affecting everything from your energy levels to your immune system's strength.

Now that we've set the stage for our genetic journey through the realm of nutrition, let's dive into the heart of the matter with a couple of real-life stories. These stories will vividly illustrate the profound impact our DNA and epigenetics can have on our nutritional choices, health, and well-being.

The Carb Coma

Meet Dennis, a forty-nine-year-old guy who, like many of us, found himself on the slippery slope of gradual weight gain. He reasoned that it was due to his age. But Dennis was determined to get to the bottom of this weight issue, so he decided to take the plunge and undergo a DNA assessment. His goal was simple: figure out why he'd been gaining weight and, more importantly, discover how to reverse this trend and regain his vitality.

His scheduled consultation was right after he had eaten lunch. That day, Dennis had indulged in a classic combo—a juicy hamburger, a pile of crispy fries, and a fizzy cola to wash it all down. As we were analyzing his DNA results, something curious happened. His eyes began to droop, and before he knew it, he was teetering on the edge of dreamland. Startling himself, Dennis snapped back to reality and profusely apologized for his sudden snooze. I couldn't help but chuckle because, thanks to his DNA report, I knew precisely what had happened—a post-carb-induced siesta.

Now, this carb sensitivity isn't a universal problem, but due to Dennis' genetic makeup, carbs triggered a rollercoaster of blood sugar spikes and crashes, often culminating in these mid-meal power naps, and he confessed that this drowsy dilemma was a frequent post-meal companion.

Armed with this newfound awareness from his DNA results, I had a simple yet powerful prescription for Dennis: embrace whole foods, bid farewell to refined carbs (those pesky processed foods and sugars), and practice mindful eating. Slow down, chew your food thoughtfully, and savor each bite.

Fast-forward three weeks, and I had the pleasure of catching up with Dennis once more. His testimonial was nothing short of glowing. Dennis had rediscovered a vitality he hadn't felt in years. His energy levels were not only restored but also sustained throughout the day. Bloating was a thing of the past, and, to top it all off, he had effortlessly shed a few pounds.

Dennis' transformation was a testament to the power of self-awareness driven by DNA insights coupled with the magic of epigenetics. It was as if he'd reclaimed the conductor's baton to his life's symphony, orchestrating a harmonious tune of health and well-being.

So, if you have ever found yourself fighting the irresistible urge to doze off after a hearty meal, let Dennis' story serve as a reminder that your unique genetic makeup can hold the keys to unlocking a healthier, more vibrant life.

Genetic Awakening: Decoding the Link between DNA and Nutrition

In early 2017, my relationship with food underwent a seismic shift. The reason? The unexpected results of my DNA assessment that revealed the complex interplay between my nutrition and my health. I often find myself wondering what might have happened if only I had this information earlier—could I have avoided the fall that shattered my Boston Marathon dreams?

Unbeknownst to me, a battle raged within, as silent inflammation wreaked havoc. This wasn't merely a byproduct of my grueling workouts or the scant hours I rested. My daily plate of food, those seemingly innocent choices, either fanned these inflammatory flames or doused them. The DNA test peeled back the layers of my ignorance, highlighting the indispensable role of antioxidant-packed berries and fruits; the sanctity of omega-3-loaded delights like salmon and the understated flaxseed; and the power-packed brigade of cruciferous veggies—cabbage, broccoli, Brussels sprouts—as warriors against inflammation.

I always enjoyed fruits, berries, and veggies. I understood the might of omega-3s. But what blindsided me? The revelation that my DNA harbored quirks. These genetic nuances hindered my body from efficiently utilizing vital micronutrients. While having certain genes doesn't guarantee deficiencies, they acted as glaring caution signs for me. Between my intense exercise schedule and DNA-driven nutrient absorption challenges, inflammation became my shadow, explaining the ceaseless fatigue, pains, and that ill-fated tumble.

But it wasn't just about inflammation. My once resilient body now demanded two-day sabbaticals between my rigorous workouts. My unyielding fitness fervor, rather than propelling me forward, was ironically becoming a health pitfall.

Reflecting now, clarity paints a vivid picture. Perhaps I could have sidestepped the constant joint pain, the crippling muscle cramps, and the fall that tore into my hip labrum. While it might not have signaled a career's end, it undoubtedly fractured a cherished piece of who I was.

In the intricate dance of genetics and nutrition, another gene emerged as a significant player: the one responsible for our body's inflammatory response. This gene can either heighten or dampen our immune system's reaction to certain triggers.

In this ongoing saga of genetics, nutrition, and health, each meal becomes a pivotal scene in our narrative—a chance to positively influence our genetic destiny. It's a story of empowerment, where we can seize control of our health through mindful choices and a deep understanding of our genetic makeup.

In the intricate dance between nutrition and DNA, certain genes have taken center stage, captivating researchers and health enthusiasts alike. I'd like to guide you through three extensively studied genetic contributors whose roles in our nutrition and overall health have proven to have significant importance: FTO, MTHFR, and CYP1A2.

But remember, while our genes offer insights, they do not dictate our destiny. Possessing a specific gene is not a conclusive fate but rather a signpost, guiding us toward informed choices. After all, our shared journey is to harness this wisdom and pave the way to a life full of vibrancy.

FTO: The "Fat Gene" Myth and Mastering Your Destiny

In the intricate world of genetics and nutrition, I uncovered a fascinating character: the FTO gene, often whimsically referred to as the "fat gene." This gene is known for its association with obesity and appetite regulation. Imagine having a gene that doesn't signal your body when it's full, so you feel perpetually unsatisfied.

Picture a plate of your favorite fatty food in front of you, and you simply can't resist having just a little more, and then a bit more, until suddenly, it's all gone. It's like being on autopilot, consuming calorie-dense, fatty foods almost mindlessly. You may have experienced this phenomenon when you're out with friends, surrounded by tempting snacks, or even during meetings when irresistible pastries beckon.

This is where the FTO gene comes into play. For those of us who have inherited this high risk gene mutation, it not only increases the likelihood of obesity, but it also affects the brain's impulse control and taste preferences. It's as if the "stop" signal gets lost in translation, leaving us more vulnerable to indulging in high-calorie, fatty foods. The result? Weight gain and a constant battle against impulsive eating.

But here's the good news: knowing about this genetic predisposition can empower you to take control. You can create strategies to outsmart your impulses, such as measuring portions or opting for smaller, more frequent meals. With self-awareness and an understanding of your unique genetic makeup, you can make choices that align with your health and vibrancy.

CYP1A2: The Tale of Two Coffee Lovers

Meet Jane and Nick, two ardent coffee aficionados. Their love for coffee was more than just its rich aroma or the artistry of latte designs; it was their morning ritual, an unspoken bond of shared silences as the dawn broke.

Every morning, they'd head to their favorite local café, Sunrise Brews. Jane would get her usual—a double espresso—while Nick always went for a tall latte. By midmorning, while Jane felt alert and energetic, Nick often complained about feeling jittery and unexpectedly anxious. He'd say, "It's just work stress," but this pattern continued, becoming almost predictable.

One day, during a casual conversation with the café's barista, they heard about the "caffeine gene"—the CYP1A2. They, too, decided to undergo DNA testing, and the results were a revelation.

Jane had the "fast" variant of the CYP1A2 gene, which allowed her to metabolize caffeine quickly. This explained her heightened alertness post her double espresso. On the other hand, Nick had the "slow" variant. His body processed caffeine at a snail's pace, leading to it staying in his system longer and causing those familiar jitters and anxious feelings.

Equipped with this new knowledge, Nick switched to a half-caffeinated blend. Over time, the jitters vanished. The morning coffee sessions remained unchanged, only now, they both savored their brews with a deeper appreciation—not just for the flavors, but also for the insights their genes had poured into their cups.

The moral? Our genes have a story to tell. Sometimes, it's as simple as how we enjoy our daily brew.

But here's the revelation: genetics may load the gun, but our lifestyle and dietary choices pull the trigger. Through our food choices, we have the power to manage and control inflammation. By selecting anti-inflammatory foods rich in antioxidants and essential nutrients, we can transform a tempestuous sea of inflammation into a serene pond of well-being.

In this ongoing saga of genetics, nutrition, and health, each meal becomes a chance to positively influence our genetic destiny. It's a story of empowerment, where we can seize control of our health through mindful choices and a deep understanding of our genetic makeup.

Crazy fact!

Your gut processes about 2.5 gallons of food daily. In an average lifespan, that's approximately sixty tons of food.[15]

Evolving Nutrition for the Wise and Vibrant Sage

True vibrancy in aging isn't just about the absence of disease, it's about radiating energy and vitality. At its heart lies the fuel we consume—our food.

What's healthy for one might not resonate with another. This isn't a one-size-fits-all approach but rather a call for personalized nutrition. While I don't advocate for hard-and-fast rules like "consume nine servings of veggies daily," some universal truths hold:

Embrace the Goodness of Nature

Eat foods as close to their natural state as possible. Did you know that biting into a fresh apple packs more nutrients than eating applesauce? The less processed a food is, the more nutrients it retains.

Moderate Sugar and Simple Carbs

Occasional indulgences won't harm, but excess sugars are often empty calories without nutritional merit.

Tread Lightly with Alcohol

Overconsumption can throw your gut's equilibrium off balance. Also, remember that alcohol, which is devoid of nutritional value, gets metabolized before anything else.

---

[15] Lillian So Chan and Manny W. Radomski, PhD, "Feel and Look Good from the Inside Out," Ixcela, accessed October 28, 2023, https://ixcela.com/resources/feel-and-look-good-from-the-inside-out.html.

Harmonize Your Plate

Balance carbs, proteins, and healthy fats. Ever felt sluggish post-pizza? Or hungry after a light salad? That's an imbalance at play.

Relish Social Eating but Stay Mindful

Guilt has no place at festive tables. Still, it's worth remembering how certain foods make you feel.

Swap the Fizz for Fizz

Eschew sodas in favor of herbal teas, water, or seltzer. If you crave a dash of sweetness, fruit-infused options, like a refreshing watermelon-basil juice, might just hit the spot.

Choose Your Oils Wisely

Some oils might be more detrimental than sugar. Prioritize olive oil, avocado oil, coconut oil, ghee, and occasional sesame oil.

Start Strong

Your breakfast sets the tone. Select nutrient-rich choices that offer sustained energy.

Listen to Your Body

Your body is constantly changing. When you feel energized, healthy, and vibrant, your cells are being properly fueled. Fundamentally, food is more nutritious the closer it is to its natural state. Consider the aftermath of a donut-laden breakfast versus one anchored in whole foods, such as an egg and avocado toast.

Keep in mind that this journey is ever-changing. We've all experienced those moments when we felt amazing, full of energy, and in the flow of life. Yet there have been times when we felt less than our best. Just as our bodies and circumstances shift, our nutritional needs adjust as well. It's like a dance, a rhythm that calls for mindfulness, adaptation, and occasionally, a fresh approach.

I believe that dis-ease is our body's way of telling us it's not well and that adjustments need to be made.

As I hope you have come to realize, there's no one-size-fits-all approach to nutrition. What nourishes you today might not be ideal tomorrow. Your gut plays a pivotal role in this ever-evolving journey.

Here is a short list of nutrient-rich foods that have stood the test of time:

Oysters, lobster, crab
Organic grass-fed beef, free-range chicken, or pork
Wild salmon, sardines, tuna, herring
Nuts—walnuts, almonds, pecans
Seeds—flax seeds, pumpkin seeds
Beets, including their greens
Watermelon
Apples
Berries (ideally organic)
Pomegranates
Dark leafy vegetables—arugula, spinach, kale
Radishes
Avocado

Feasting on Life: Nourishment beyond the Plate

Eating is far more than just counting calories or following the latest diet trend. It's all about connection—to our bodies, to the earth, and to the rhythm of life itself. Every morsel we consume carries a story of its origin, and in turn, it becomes part of our story.

There's an old saying: You are what you eat. But I'd like to propose a new saying: You become the energy of what you consume. Think of each bite as an infusion of vitality, a chance to reshape, rejuvenate, and reinvigorate your body.

With this insight into the interplay between genes and nutrition in mind, I sought expert insights into the world of holistic nutrition. This pursuit led to an enlightening conversation with a naturopathic doctor, Dr. Karl Goldkamp.

Unexpected Lessons at the Lunch Buffet

I've always prided myself on my open-mindedness, but it was a Sunday in 2019 when I learned that biases—especially about food—could be more deep-seated than I thought.

At a three-day Healthpreneur conference, filled with professionals exchanging knowledge, I had the opportunity to meet and collaborate with Dr. Karl Goldkamp (Dr. Karl) and his wife. The conference, tailored for entrepreneurs in the health and wellness space, provided the perfect backdrop for our encounter. Come lunchtime, the spread was as expected—fresh, organic, and a nutritionist's dream come true.

But as I queued behind Dr. Karl, his plate caught my attention—it was an anomaly. Piled high with only meats and shrimp, it looked starkly different from everyone else's "balanced" plates.

Curiosity nudged me. I ventured, "Why only protein?"

"I'm a carnivore," he replied, his statement punctuated with a smile that hinted at a story worth hearing.

His journey was anything but ordinary. Dr. Karl had once thrived on a plant-centric diet, even cultivating over half an acre of organic produce. But a tumultuous period marked by personal loss and health challenges forced him to rethink everything.

The challenges he faced from 2008 to 2010 were formidable: financial upheavals, losing loved ones, being diagnosed with ulcerative colitis and Crohn's disease, and his wife's harrowing health ordeal. It wasn't just about changing diets; it was about reclaiming life.

Diving deep into research, Dr. Karl found hope in the ketogenic diet. He pivoted from a diet of over 90 percent plant-based to a diet that was nearly all meat-based. It might sound extreme, but the results spoke volumes. Today, he's a testament to the belief that there isn't a one-size-fits-all in nutrition.

An Insightful Conversation with a Wellness Maverick

Let me introduce you to Karl Goldkamp, a true wellness maverick and a naturopathic doctor with a treasure trove of credentials: ND, L.Ac., Dipl OM, and certified in environmental medicine. He is also a certified expert in Chinese herbal medicine. Karl is not just a practitioner; he's a pioneer.

Dr. Karl was the first student in his university's history to earn two degrees simultaneously: a doctorate in naturopathy and a master's in acupuncture. His journey didn't stop there; in fact, it was just the beginning.

With a significant presence in the digital realm, Dr. Karl commands attention through his influential Facebook group, a thought-provoking podcast, and an enlightening YouTube series. He's a wellness trailblazer, and my conversation with him uncovered pearls of wisdom about vibrant aging and the power of nutrition.

Q: Could you offer some insights into your journey and experience in the field of nutrition and holistic health?

I am a naturopathic doctor with over sixteen years of experience. I consider myself as having more than adequate intelligence, as shown by completing two programs from Bastyr University. I went back to medical school in my midthirties. During this time, I only focused on medical school so that I could give one hundred percent.

Q: Could you share some of your journey?

For over a decade, I had a very successful practice in Connecticut—in fact, my wife and I even had an entire medical building. We lived a very healthy lifestyle. At that time, we ate primarily a plant-based diet. We had a huge organic garden. It must have been at least half an acre. We grew many different types of fruits and vegetables, including grapes and kiwis. We only grew produce that was easy. If the produce tended to have bug issues, we didn't plant it. We were also big into fresh herbs. All was going well until 2008. It was a catastrophe. Do you know why? You could hear a pin drop. People weren't even doing their copays. The financial struggles began. I had to eventually file for bankruptcy. The next two years were filled with personal struggles. My mother and brother died. Then my wife was diagnosed with melanoma, right by her optic nerve, which required a thirteen-hour brain surgery. And so, she then did lose her vision in one eye. I wasn't certain she would survive. Thankfully, I can say she is now doing well and is very healthy. Nonetheless, with all the stress, my gut just exploded.

Q: Your gut exploded?

I couldn't eat anything. The pain was so great. I lost a tremendous amount of weight. My family was concerned that I was dying. A colonoscopy revealed ulcerative colitis and Crohn's disease. My body was not absorbing nutrients.

Q: What did you do?

I started with the conventional medical system and did what I was told. However, I was put on the wrong medications, which gave me anemia down to a hemoglobin of a medical grade of fifteen, which should be forty-five. I was at death's door and not getting the attention I deserved. I was weeks away from potential death. It was at this point I recognized that I had to take back the responsibility for my health.

Q: How did you go about getting back your health?

It was challenging. I was so tired. As a scientist and researcher, I read books and journals. I got off my medication. My colleagues made suggestions, which included probiotics and herbs. I got marginally better. I knew there had to be more to heal my gut and regain my health. Slowly, I regained enough strength to travel internationally, in Europe and Australia, for medical conferences on gastrointestinal, GI health. This research and study ultimately led me to explore and embrace what is referred to as the ketogenic diet.

Q: How did you make the transition to a ketogenic diet?

Bone broth was the first remedy and the only food I could have. From there, I started learning about ketosis. This is two years before the ketogenic movement, and far before exogenous ketones. Slowly, I began to replace vegetables with meat and healthy fats. It worked, and now I have regained my health and vitality. In fact, today I no longer have a diagnosis of ulcerative colitis or Crohn's disease.

Q: Is this why you launched your *Keto Naturopath with Dr. Karl Goldkamp* podcast?

Absolutely! I had really screwed up my own health, and now that I had discovered how I could heal my gut, my body, I wanted to share this knowledge to help others. I wanted to let people know that even as a professional, I struggled. I almost died. Now I share my knowledge and lessons every week on my podcast.

Q: What did you eat prior to 2008? What was your lifestyle like?

At the time, approximately ninety percent of our diet consisted of nonmeat proteins, even though we did eat meat. If we were ninety percent then, currently we're ninety-nine percent protein to one percent nonprotein. I wouldn't say I was a vegetarian. I mean, we ate meat once a week. It was a big change, going from primarily vegetarian to carnivore.

Q: What are your current eating habits?

My wife and I have transitioned from a purely ketogenic diet to a somewhat less strict regimen, leaning more toward a protein-sparing modified diet. This change has resulted in me achieving a leaner and healthier state than I've experienced in years. Throughout my career as a doctor, I have always placed a significant emphasis on laboratory tests to check my own health. Contrary to any misconceptions, my recent lab results are excellent, and they serve as a valuable indicator of my internal health.

Q: What about all the nutrients contained in fruits and vegetables? Aren't you missing out on those?

Years ago, I was told that whatever the animal eats, you get those nutrients too. I thought the person was ignorant. Yet years later, I realized I was the ignorant one. It is actually true that you can gain valuable plant nutrients when eating meat. You just need to eat the things that eat the greens. But it is very important to have a good, reputable, local source for meat.

Q: How do you feel about your health today compared to years ago?

In high school, I played soccer and lacrosse and swam. After high school, I became a triathlete. In July 2024, I will be sixty-eight, and I am at my high school weight. It's amazing to have that vitality back, considering I was so sick at one point. There's a truism in medicine that says if you really want to learn about health or be healthy, have a chronic disease, meaning that you now have a measurement, whether it's asthma or Crohn's. You now have a new warning system.

Q: Wow, you have shared some amazing self-awareness.

I wish I had known thirty years ago what I know now. But that wouldn't have happened, because my greatest teacher has come from being very sick and nothing helped. This self-awareness and drive to discover how to heal myself was key. I learned more from this experience than from being a smart guy in medical school who completed three different programs.

Q: Where should a person who wants to eat healthier start?

Eat whole, real foods. Avoid processed foods. While this type of lifestyle works for my wife and myself, it is not for everyone. You need to find what is best for you, your body, and your health.

Q: It must have been very challenging to change your mindset after decades as a doctor and essentially a plant-based lifestyle.

It was extremely difficult. It is a process that takes time and a commitment to self-discovery and self-awareness. For real, lasting change, there has to be a level of self-awareness that wants to get stronger. And if your why is strong, you are better able to root that new belief more deeply and more sustainably into your future. That's where I am.

Q: What do you think is the greatest mistake people make when it comes to their own nutrition?

Processed foods. The further a food is from its source, the more processed it is. Even dairy, which I do not consume, most people are not aware is ultraprocessed. Cheese is processed. It is estimated that at least sixty percent of an American's diet is processed.

Q: Thank you, Dr. Karl, for all your insights.

You're very welcome.

After this enlightening conversation with Dr. Karl, it's clear that the transformative power of nutrition and the importance of listening to our bodies cannot be underestimated. Dr. Karl's odyssey challenges conventional dietary beliefs and underscores the significance of self-awareness and adaptation when it comes to our health.

As you reflect on Dr. Karl's remarkable journey, you'll discover a treasure trove of wisdom in what I refer to as "Karlisms." Most of the wisdom was included within this interview; however, I have included additional pearls of wisdom he shared during subsequent conversations.

These are not mere words; they are profound insights that provide a roadmap to vibrant aging and optimal well-being. Each Karlism is a stepping stone on our path to unlocking the secrets of nutrition, genetics, and the art of thriving as we age. So, guided by Karl's invaluable wisdom, let's utilize the following Karlisms to crack the code to vibrant aging through nutrition.

If things are a problem, let's get around the problem.

Dr. Karl's pragmatism was clear in this simple yet powerful statement. He didn't let obstacles deter him; instead, he found innovative ways to overcome them. It was a reminder that solutions often lie just beyond our challenges.

I have to get my life back or else . . .

Dr. Karl's determination to reclaim his health was palpable in these words. It was a declaration of his unwavering commitment to self-care and a stark reminder that our well-being is ultimately in our own hands.

How I take care of myself is up to me.

This acknowledgment of personal responsibility resonated deeply. Karl understood that true well-being begins with self-care and self-awareness, emphasizing that we have the power to shape our destinies.

If you really want to learn about health or being healthy, have a chronic disease.

Dr. Karl's insight into the value of health lessons learned through adversity was eye-opening. It highlighted the role of chronic diseases as potent teachers, offering us valuable insights into our bodies and our paths to wellness.

Chronic disease is a warning system.

His perspective on chronic diseases as warning signals underscored the importance of watching our health diligently. It encouraged us to view these conditions as opportunities for improvement.

You have to pay attention to yourself.

Dr. Karl's emphasis on self-awareness was a recurring theme throughout our conversation. It served as a gentle nudge, reminding us to listen to our bodies and heed the messages they send.

My discovery was driven by self-awareness, but this self-awareness had to come from being very sick and saying, Whatever you are doing now is not working for you.

Dr. Karl's personal revelation highlighted the transformational power of self-awareness, especially when driven by necessity. It encouraged us to be open to change and self-discovery.

New habits need to know why—rooting beliefs into the future.

Dr. Karl's insight into the importance of understanding the "why" behind new habits was profound. It urged us to anchor our beliefs deeply, ensuring lasting and meaningful change.

People do not come to health out of curiosity; they usually come to health out of pain and/or crisis. They have to hurt.

This sobering truth reminded us that often, it takes discomfort or a crisis to motivate us to prioritize our health. It encouraged us to act before pain becomes our driving force.

Motivation is pain.

Dr. Karl's blunt statement underscored the power of pain as a motivator for change. It challenged us to find sources of motivation beyond discomfort and pain, driving us toward healthier choices.

If you jump too far too fast, you will just rebound and then say it didn't work.

His caution against rapid, drastic changes served as a valuable reminder. It encouraged us to take measured steps toward our health goals, reducing the risk of setbacks.

By being very sick, you let go of all the head trash and what others think.

Dr. Karl's experience highlighted the liberation that often comes with illness. It reminded us to shed self-limiting beliefs and external pressures, focusing on what truly matters—our health.

There has to be a degree of self-awareness that wants to get healthy.

Karl's final Karlism served as a poignant conclusion. It encapsulated the essence of our conversation—a call to embrace self-awareness, transformation, and ultimately, vibrant aging.

These Karlisms are not just words on a page; they are guides to unlocking the secrets of vibrant aging through nutrition. They are a testament to the resilience of the human spirit and the power we each hold to shape our destiny.

Meeting Dr. Karl transformed my understanding of food, nutrition, and well-being. Have you ever sized up people based on their plates? I certainly had. But that day, as I stood in line at the buffet, his plate challenged my preconceived notions, leading to profound insights about what constitutes good health. His story is a reminder that health isn't just about what's on our plates; it's also about understanding why it's there.

Please see the Acknowledgments and Contact Information section at the end of the book for more details about Dr. Karl.

Cracking the Code to Vibrant Aging through Nutrition

In this chapter, we dived deep into the intricate relationship between nutrition, our gut, and our DNA. Beyond calorie counting, we explored the profound link between our dietary choices and our genetic makeup.

Highlighting the significance of genes like MTHFR and FTO, we learned that while genes may influence our predisposition, they don't determine our destiny. Dr. Karl's journey demonstrates that what's nutritious for one may not hold true for another, especially as we age.

The importance of nutrient-dense foods and a diet that aligns with nature's offerings was emphasized. Processed foods, sugars, and excessive alcohol were discouraged, while the virtues of a balanced intake of carbs, proteins, and healthy fats were celebrated. Social gatherings became occasions for mindful eating.

Our perspective shifted from calorie counting to a holistic approach, focusing on our body's ability to absorb and use nutrients. Listening to our body, interpreting its signals, and meeting its unique needs became the keys to unlocking vibrant aging.

Moving forward, let food be our ally—a source of joy, energy, and profound connection. Cherish each bite, each flavor, and each moment of nourishment as a celebration of life's vibrancy.

So, with that in mind, *how will you nourish your body to support your path to vibrant aging?*

Now, on to Pillar Four: sleep. This is often underestimated, but it's a powerful force that rejuvenates our body and mind and plays a vital role in crafting a vibrant existence.

CHAPTER 7

PILLAR FOUR

QUALITY SLEEP: TIME TO RECHARGE YOUR CELLS

> *Sleep is that golden chain that ties health and our bodies together.*
> — THOMAS DEKKER

In the quiet embrace of the night, as the world slumbers, a remarkable transformation takes place within you. You don't notice it happening; it's only when you wake up that you realize how good you feel. Sleep, the fourth pillar of health, holds a profound power over our well-being, yet we often neglect it.

Do you prioritize your sleep?

If you're like me, you've been inconsistent at best.

In my own life, the first three decades were a sleepless blur. I was blissfully unaware of the impact of a good night's sleep on my well-being. Staying up late to meet a deadline or partying with friends was par for the course. Sure, I'd wake up tired, but I soldiered on without much thought.

In my twenties, I seemed to possess an endless reservoir of energy to compensate for wild nights out. While I recognized the importance of sleep, it rarely deterred me. However, that's no longer the case. Today, a single night of poor sleep can wreak havoc on my energy, vitality, and performance.

Can you recall a pivotal event, situation, or health issue that forced you to confront the importance of sleep?

In the first chapter, I shared the struggles I had during my midthirties when neurological symptoms led me to seek an assessment by a top multiple sclerosis specialist in New York. As it turned out, my symptoms were primarily attributed to stress. What I didn't delve into at that time was the parallel battle I was fighting with sleep. Perhaps this part of my story will resonate with you too.

Picture this: you're lying in bed, but racing thoughts relentlessly echo in your mind, preventing you from slipping into slumber. Or perhaps, like me, you manage to doze off, only to awaken a few hours later with a swarm of thoughts buzzing about the tasks awaiting you the next day. Does this nighttime mental marathon sound all too familiar?

Even before meeting with the multiple sclerosis specialist, I understood that sleep played a pivotal role in my overall well-being. A single night of poor sleep, whether due to late-night deadlines or early-morning parenting duties, sent me into a tailspin. Fatigue became my constant companion, and the challenges of the day seemed insurmountable. Simple tasks drained me, and I couldn't ignore the alarming difficulty I faced with word recall—a particularly distressing issue for someone working as a speech pathologist.

In the wake of that period when I was overstretched, I inadvertently stumbled upon a hidden treasure that had always been right before my eyes: the invaluable gift of a good night's sleep. It took some time for me to truly grasp its significance, but once I did, I experienced a profound awakening. This elusive state became the cornerstone of my rejuvenation, effectively alleviating my troubling symptoms. After nearly three decades since that revelation, I've made a steadfast commitment to prioritize sleep. Through this process, I've learned that when sleep falters, so does my immune system, making me susceptible to infections and illnesses. It became abundantly clear that my body doesn't work optimally without the restorative power of adequate sleep.

So, do you find yourself sensitive to the slightest disruptions in your sleep routine? Do you have nights when sleep eludes you, and the next day feels like an uphill battle, affecting your energy, mood, and performance?

Let's examine the significance of sleep and its profound effects on our lives. As you read on, think about how many hours of restful sleep you truly need each night and how your energy and vitality are intimately linked to your sleep quality.

Sleep doesn't just impact individuals like me; it profoundly influences the performance and recovery of those I've had the privilege to work with throughout my career. Take, for example, the adults with neurological disorders I worked with during my years as a speech pathologist. In their world, sleep wasn't just about getting through the night; it was the key to unlocking their potential each day.

Picture this: one day, a client's word retrieval skills are sharp, their speech clarity is on point, and their comprehension and problem-solving abilities are firing on all cylinders. The next day, after a night of restless sleep, it's as if those cognitive gears have ground to a halt. Can you relate to the fluctuations in your energy levels throughout the day, from feeling like the Energizer Bunny to feeling sluggish like a snail?

Now, as a personal trainer, I've seen firsthand the impact sleep has on exercise performance—not just in my clients but in myself as well. It's a phenomenon I'm eager to share with you because it's not just about the quantity of sleep; it's about the quality too.

A good night's sleep enhances your cardiovascular system, improving blood flow and respiration. These are essential for any exercise regimen. When it comes to strength training, which requires focus and power, fatigue is a formidable opponent. Your cells struggle to generate the necessary power for lifting weights and sustaining movements when you're sleep-deprived.

Balance, arguably the most affected aspect of physical performance when you're tired, underpins all movements except sitting and lying down. Imagine the impact of sleep deprivation on your ability to maintain balance or complete the one-legged balance test.

Have you ever noticed the difference in your exercise performance on days when you're well-rested versus days when you're sleep-deprived?

It's a gap you can feel but might not fully understand. While exercise might momentarily boost your energy after a restless night, it's no substitute for the revitalization of a good night's sleep. As we dive deeper into the world of sleep, you'll discover that it's the cornerstone of vitality and cellular function, and its influence reaches far beyond the gym.

Do your cravings for certain foods, like carbs, surge when you're sleep-deprived?

It's a phenomenon I've experienced, even as someone who doesn't particularly favor carbohydrates. The allure of a scone or muffin becomes irresistible when fatigue sets in. Yet, an hour later, you find yourself yearning for a nap.

The pursuit of sustained energy, vital for connecting with others and finding happiness, hinges on getting the sleep and rest your body craves.

But before we get into the specifics of sleep, have you ever come across someone who boasts about needing only a few hours of sleep? Let's address this myth together.

Mary's Journey to Restful Nights: How Sleep Transformed Her Life

Mary, a woman in her early forties, had been a regular attendee in my exercise classes. However, she felt a renewed determination to prioritize her health and well-being. During our first consultation, I asked her a simple question: "Do you sleep through the night?"

With matter-of-fact candor, Mary responded, "I haven't slept through the night since I was pregnant with my son ten years ago. Lack of sleep is now part of my life, and I've grown accustomed to it."

Can you fathom enduring a decade without the luxury of a solid night's sleep?

Initially, Mary's focus for health coaching centered around weight loss. Recognizing the profound link between weight and sleep, I saw this as both the perfect starting point and an opportunity for lasting change. But as she shared further details, Mary revealed the complexities of her life, which were a relentless whirlwind of stress and ceaseless mental chatter.

As a devoted mother, wife, and full-time professional, Mary was perpetually juggling her myriad roles, often pushing self-care to the lowest priority. Sleep, in her eyes, was a time-consuming indulgence. Her plan, as she shared, was to catch up on her sleep once her child left for college.

Here's an unsettling truth: Suffering from continuous sleep debt or chronic sleep deprivation significantly heightens the chances of developing conditions such as diabetes, hypertension, heart disease, and stroke. Furthermore, sleep deprivation is closely associated with diminished immune function, disrupted metabolism leading to weight gain, and an increased susceptibility to falls and accidents. Prolonged sleep deprivation also exerts a profound impact on memory and cognitive abilities.

It became glaringly obvious that sleep deprivation had cast a shadow over every area of Mary's existence: her health, emotional well-being, work performance, and relationships with loved ones. Chronic fatigue, as we all know, has the power to extinguish our vibrancy and passion. It's simply impossible to thrive under such circumstances.

Mary approached our sessions with a mix of excitement and skepticism, unsure if anything could truly alleviate her sleep struggles. Nonetheless, she was determined to try. So I suggested two simple steps to take for the following week:

Purposeful Breathing

I encouraged Mary to cultivate mindfulness around her breath, using its profound ability to soothe the body and activate the parasympathetic nervous system—often referred to as the "rest and digest system." Throughout the day, she practiced taking deep, calming breaths as needed. Before bed, she devoted thirty minutes to focused, slow, and deep breathing to promote relaxation and better sleep.

Embracing Electronic Detox

Mary committed to powering down all devices and electronics at least sixty minutes before bedtime.

Even I, as her coach, was pleasantly surprised when Mary returned the following week, her face radiating with delight. She had already enjoyed a couple nights of over seven hours of restful sleep. Her newfound enthusiasm for improving her health was palpable.

Are you, like Mary, trapped in the cycle of sleep deprivation, resigned to the notion that a good night's sleep is a distant memory?

While it's widely recognized that sleep is crucial for both physical and mental well-being, its true significance is often underestimated or overlooked. Let's discover how sleep can transform your life, just as it did for Mary.

Unlocking the Mysteries of Sleep: Unveiling the Secret Forces that Fuel Cellular Renewal and Empower Vibrant Aging

In a world brimming with information, sleep is the one essential topic that often remains in the shadows, quietly shaping our lives. We might not think about it much, especially if we're fortunate enough to enjoy restful nights, but sleep is far from a luxury—it's a fundamental necessity. In fact, there are over 273,000 studies on sleep in the PubMed database, with many of them emerging in recent decades.

Here are six pivotal reasons why sleep is the unsung hero of cellular repair and rejuvenation:

Restoring the Symphony of Circadian Rhythm

Just as a conductor leads an orchestra, your body follows its own rhythm—the circadian rhythm. This rhythm orchestrates your heart, digestion, and even hormones like cortisol. Ever felt your energy fluctuate during the day or noticed monthly hormonal changes? These rhythms are vital, and they're orchestrated by sleep.

Hormonal Harmony

Hormones aren't merely responsible for physical changes; they hold the key to our emotional well-being, energy levels, and even our weight. Your body's hormonal dance is guided by the circadian rhythm. Think of hormones as chemical messengers, intricately woven into the fabric of your well-being.

Melatonin, the Sleep Regulator

The hormone melatonin, the guardian of sleep, steps onto the stage when darkness falls. It signals your cells that it's time to prepare for slumber. In today's world of perpetual brightness, melatonin often struggles to take its cue, resulting in poor sleep quality.

Purging Stress and Clutter

Life's stresses bombard our brains daily. Picture your brain as a storage bin, overflowing with information and worries. During restorative sleep, these "stimuli" are neatly organized and discarded, leaving your mind clear and ready for a new day. Inadequate sleep leaves these bins cluttered, affecting your emotional balance.

Cellular Cleansing

While you rest, your cells engage in a meticulous cleaning process. They clear the accumulated "garbage" from the stresses you face daily. Sleep is like a reset button that recalibrates your body and mind. Sleep is imperative for your cells to function optimally and for them to be more vibrant and youthful. If your cells aren't healthy, neither are you.

Magic in the Night

As you slumber, especially during deep rapid eye movement (REM) sleep, your cells are tirelessly working to process the day's "garbage." If sleep eludes you, both you and your cells are out of sync, and you'll wake up feeling less than vibrant.

Let's expand on each of these facets and explore the intricate tapestry of sleep's impact on our cellular vitality and becoming a vibrant sage.

Circadian Rhythm: Your Body's Built-In Timekeeper and Hormonal Maestro

Your body is a precision-engineered system with its own built-in timing mechanism known as the circadian rhythm. This internal timing system regulates essential functions like your heartbeat, digestion, and hormonal activity, ensuring seamless coordination between various processes throughout your day.

Let's take a closer look at how this works.

Imagine waking up in the morning feeling energized. This is when cortisol, often known as the stress hormone, takes the stage, giving you that initial boost to start your day. As the day progresses, cortisol gradually steps aside, making room for other hormones and rhythms.

Now, when you hear the word "hormones," what comes to mind? Weight fluctuations, mood swings, or maybe your energy levels? Hormones are like the backstage crew behind the scenes of your daily life. They influence everything from your emotions to your appetite.

Here's the intriguing part: your hormones dance to the beat of your circadian rhythm. This rhythm is like your body's internal clock, ticking away over a twenty-four-hour cycle, balancing rest and activity. While we all share some basic rhythms, each of us has a unique pattern, much like a fingerprint. But just as your body has its rhythm, your cells have their own rhythm too. These cellular rhythms play a vital role in orchestrating your hormones, making sure everything runs smoothly.

Imagine hormones as messengers carrying important instructions. They travel through your bloodstream to different parts of your body, affecting these processes:

Growth and Development

They help you grow and mature.

Metabolism

They control how your body turns food into energy.

Sexual Function

They influence your romantic desires.

Reproduction

They're in charge of the complex process of creating life.

Mood

They have a say in how you feel from moment to moment.

Unlocking the Mysteries of Melatonin: Your Body's Hidden Elixir of Youth

In the depths of your brain, nestled within the pineal gland, exists a remarkable substance—a silent guardian of your health, your sleep, and your vitality. Its name is melatonin, and it might just be the key to unlocking the secrets of vibrant aging.

Picture this: as the sun dips below the horizon, your body starts a meticulously orchestrated symphony. Melatonin, your body's natural timekeeper, takes center stage. With each passing minute of darkness, its production gradually increases, signaling your entire body that it's time to rest, rejuvenate, and heal. Melatonin, often referred to as the "hormone of darkness," is your body's way of saying, The world may be awake, but it's your time to dream.

Yet in our modern, bustling world, where artificial lights shine brightly into the wee hours and disrupt the natural rhythm of night and day, melatonin often struggles to make its grand entrance. The consequences are profound and far-reaching. As melatonin's nightly performance falters, so does our ability to experience the kind of deep, restorative sleep that defies the ravages of time.

But melatonin is not merely a sleep regulator; it's also a guardian of youth. Within its molecules lies a potent secret—a remarkable ability to combat the aging process itself. As an antioxidant, melatonin tirelessly shields your cells from the relentless assaults of oxidative stress, which is the driving force behind the aging process.

Imagine melatonin as a sentinel stationed at the front lines of your body's defenses. While you slumber, it's on a mission to repair, restore, and rejuvenate. It scavenges the free radicals that threaten to corrode your cells and tissues and ensures that your body awakens each morning as a fresher, more vibrant version of itself.

But melatonin's role doesn't stop there. It's your body's immune system's closest confidant, bolstering its defenses and standing ready to fend off invaders. As you age, maintaining a robust immune response becomes increasingly vital. Melatonin, the ageless guardian, plays an irreplaceable role in this battle.

So, as you ponder the mysteries of melatonin, consider that perhaps the secret to timeless vibrancy isn't found in a fountain of youth or a miraculous elixir. Instead, it might be concealed within the delicate balance of lightness and darkness and the magic woven into the fabric of your circadian rhythm.

Tonight, when you lay your head to rest, remember that melatonin is more than just a sleep aid; it's the conductor of the symphony of your life. It orchestrates the dance of your cells, the melody of your dreams, and the harmony of your health. Cherish this natural elixir, for in its embrace, you may find the key to a more vibrant, more youthful you.

Reclaiming Your Inner Sanctuary: The Art of Stress Reduction and Cellular Cleansing

Stress is an undeniable part of life. From the moment you wake up, your brain is constantly processing a whirlwind of stimuli and information, navigating the complexities of daily existence. Picture your mind as a colossal storage bin, diligently collecting the events, encounters, and worries of the day. By the time you lay your head on the pillow, this mental container is filled to the brim with the stimulation of the past hours, the echoes of past concerns, and the looming specters of tomorrow's challenges.

Now, close your eyes and envision something truly transformative. Imagine a restful night of sleep as a grand cleansing ritual, a profound act of decluttering for your mind. During these precious hours, your brain undergoes a remarkable transformation. The accumulated "stimuli" are methodically sorted, and the weight of worries is gently lifted. This mental tidying empties the storage bin so that when you wake up, your mind emerges as a fresh, clear canvas, ready for the new day.

However, when sleep is elusive and those coveted seven hours of slumber remain out of reach, our "bins" don't empty as they should. The consequences are palpable and profound, affecting not only our cognitive clarity but also our emotional equilibrium.

As you slumber, something extraordinary takes place within your body's inner sanctum—the cells become diligent custodians, working to get rid of the day's accumulated "garbage." It's a process akin to cellular cleansing—a detoxification ritual of unparalleled importance.

But what exactly is this garbage? Stress, both physical and mental, is an inescapable part of our daily lives. These stressors leave an indelible mark on our cellular health—a silent toll that can't be ignored. Stress, you see, is not intrinsically good or bad; it's all about balance—a delicate recalibration of your body and mind.

And here's a thought-provoking statistic: Adults who fall short of the recommended sleep duration are more likely to report chronic health conditions.[16] This revelation underscores the profound impact of sleep on our overall well-being, extending far beyond mere fatigue.

But there's more to this story. Did you know that a chronic lack of sleep may even increase your vulnerability to developing dementia? It's a stark reminder of the crucial role sleep plays in preserving our cognitive health as we age.

Now, let's explore the remarkable process of detoxification—a metabolic marvel through which toxins are transmuted into less

---

16 Séverine Sabia et al., "Association of Sleep Duration at Age 50, 60, and 70 Years with Risk of Multimorbidity in the UK: 25-Year Follow-Up of the Whitehall II Cohort Study," PLOS Medicine, October 18, 2022, accessed April 16, 2024, https://journals.plos.org/plosmedicine/article?id=10.1371/journal.pmed.1004109.

harmful substances, primed for excretion. In essence, detoxification is your body's way of discarding the cellular garbage collected throughout the day.

Sleep Emerges as the Unsung Hero of Detoxification

To aid in this intricate detox dance, you have your trusty mitochondria—the tiny cellular powerhouses responsible for producing energy. Among their many duties, mitochondria play a pivotal role in dismantling and getting rid of the excess oxygen in our cells, a process known as oxidative stress. This cleansing action is essential, deciding whether cells wither away as old and spent or appear as new, youthful, and vibrant.

So remember that within the embrace of a restful night's sleep lies not just the promise of a clear mind and refreshed body but the profound act of cellular cleansing and the preservation of your inner sanctuary. Cherish your sleep, for it is the key to unlocking the doors of a healthier, more vibrant you.

Now that you have a deeper understanding of sleep's profound influence on hormones, cellular repair, and the aging process, let's look at the intricate connection between sleep and our overall health. The research has been very strong in concluding that lack of sleep, especially over an extended period of time, has a significant negative impact on overall health. While there have been many studies, it's still hard to understand why this is so. This section highlights some of the most prevalent factors based on current research and studies.

Heart Health, Sleep, and Immunity: The Inflammation Connection

Imagine for a moment the delicate dance between sleep and your heart. It's a relationship where each partner influences the other and can either elevate your health to new heights or send it spiraling down a treacherous path. So, the simple yet profound question is: What comes first—poor sleep or poor health?

Enter the American Heart Association (AHA) journal entitled *Circulation*, where a groundbreaking study illuminated the importance of sleep patterns on our heart's destiny. Astonishingly, it reported that individuals with the healthiest sleep routines boasted a remarkable 42 percent lower risk of heart failure, independent of other risk factors.[17]

What's even more fascinating is how sleep's magical touch extends beyond its role in heart health. You've already discovered that while you slumber, your body engages in a meticulous cleanup operation, tidying up the debris of the day and ensuring your mind is fresh for a new dawn. But here's a revelation that might astonish you: a good night's sleep also acts as a guardian for your arteries, battling against inflammation and clearing away the built-up waste.

Inflammation, often the instigator of common diseases, is a formidable foe. However, according to *Medical News Today*, a well-rested body helps to maintain the suppleness of your arteries, thwarting the dreaded hardening that can lead to heart issues.[18] In fact, research from the University of Colorado at Boulder has unraveled the intricate connection between insufficient sleep and the buildup of fatty deposits in our arteries, a process known as atherogenesis. This, in turn, heightens the risk of strokes and heart attacks, casting a shadow on our heart's health.[19]

---

17 Penny M. Kris-Etherton et al., "Strategies for Promotion of a Healthy Lifestyle in Clinical Settings: Pillars of Ideal Cardiovascular Health: A Science Advisory From the American Heart Association," *Circulation*, October 25, 2021, accessed March 15, 2024, https://www.ahajournals.org/doi/epub/10.1161/CIR.0000000000001018.

18 Adam Felman, "Everything You Need to Know about Heart Disease," *Medical News Today*, October 26, 2023, accessed April 12, 2024, https://www.medicalnewstoday.com/articles/23719.

19 Lisa Marshall, "Why Lack of Sleep is Bad for Your Heart," University of Colorado Boulder, May 20, 2019, https://www.colorado.edu/today/2019/05/20/why-lack-sleep-bad-your-heart.

So, consider this a profound revelation: every night, as you sink into slumber, your heart and sleep collaborate to influence not only your rest but also your heart's vigor. It's a symphony worth orchestrating for a vibrant, heart-healthy life.

Unlocking the Secrets of Sleep and Passion

Ah, the mysteries of sleep and passion—a topic that's intriguing and maybe even a little playful. Let's examine the intriguing connection between your slumber and your desires.

For men, the phenomenon known as "morning wood" is more than just a quirky wake-up call. It serves as a vital indicator of overall health. A noticeable absence of this natural occurrence might signal issues with testosterone levels, blood flow, or even more serious health concerns.

Now, what about the ladies? While research in this area is still budding, there are some intriguing findings. Just like their male counterparts, a woman who enjoys a good night's sleep and is healthy may find her clitoris becoming more aroused in the morning—a delightful revelation.

Here are a few surprising clinical insights:

1. 37 percent of women have experienced sleep-induced orgasms. Sufficient sleep has a positive impact on genital arousal. Healthy sleep patterns promote robust sexual desire, genital response, and the likelihood of engaging in partnered sexual activities.[20]
2. An added sixty to ninety minutes of sleep per night can work wonders for your happiness and overall health.[21]

---

[20] Madlen Davies, "Have You Had a 'Sleep Orgasm'? 37% of Women Have Climaxed While Dreaming, While Only Half Regularly Do during Marital Sex," *Daily Mirror*, December 15, 2015, accessed September 24, 2023, https://www.dailymail.co.uk/health/article-3359093/Have-sleep-orgasm-37-women-climaxed-dreaming-half-regularly-marital-sex.html.

[21] "More Sleep Would Make Us Happier, Healthier and Safer," American Psychological Association, 2014, accessed June 12, 2023, www.apa.org/topics/sleep/deprivation-consequences.

3. Individuals getting only five to six hours of sleep are 4.2 times more likely to catch a cold compared to those enjoying seven or more hours of sleep.[22]
4. Fifty to seventy million US adults grapple with sleep disorders.[23]
5. Chronic sleep deprivation, often linked to sleep disorders, can lead to erectile dysfunction (ED).[24]

So, whether it's the allure of a passionate night or the intrigue of sound sleep, one thing is clear: these elements play an integral role in living a vibrant and passionate life. Much like the other pillars of health, your choices today set the stage for a remarkable tomorrow, extending your health span as you age.

So, dear reader, how many hours of blissful slumber do you enjoy each night? Do you rise feeling refreshed and invigorated?

If you find yourself among the 35 percent of adults who fall short of the recommended seven hours of daily sleep, it's no wonder that feeling vibrant and at your absolute best seems elusive. Think back to those restful vacations you've cherished in your life. What made them so rejuvenating? What insights can you glean from those tranquil nights of rest to craft sleep habits that will envelop you in a deep, revitalizing slumber?

As I contemplate the miracles that unfold in our bodies during sleep, one word springs to mind: Extraordinary! Sleep is the ultimate body and organ restorer, helping "auto recovery" from disease, injury, and illness. It's essential for all aspects of life, and

---

[22] Lisa Marie Potter and Nicholas Weiler, "Short Sleepers Are Four Times More Likely to Catch a Cold," University of California, San Francisco, August 31, 2015, accessed November 14, 2023, www.ucsf.edu/news/2015/08/131411/short-sleepers-are-four-times-more-likely-catch-cold.

[23] Institute of Medicine (US) Committee on Sleep Medicine and Research, "Sleep Disorders and Sleep Deprivation: An Unmet Public Health Problem," edited by Harvey R. Colten and Bruce M. Altevogt (Washington, DC: National Academies Press, 2006), accessed February 7, 2024, www.pubmed.ncbi.nlm.nih.gov/20669438.

[24] Rachel Sacks, "Can Lack of Sleep Cause Erectile Dysfunction?" reviewed by Katelyn Hagerty, FNP, Hims, November 22, 2022, accessed November 15, 2023, www.hims.com/blog/lack-of-sleep-erectile-dysfunction.

especially for your cells to do their job properly. If you're a great sleeper, that's awesome—keep up the good night's sleep habit!

Sobering statistic: After seventeen hours without sleep, your alertness levels mimic those of a person with a blood alcohol concentration of 0.05 percent, which, under US law, falls into the "impaired" category.[25]

Unlocking the Secrets of Sleep: A Conversation with Allison Brager, PhD

As I've journeyed through the pillars of health, I've come to appreciate the profound significance of sleep and the role it plays not only for daily vibrancy but for long-term well-being and aging. To provide you with the most up-to-date insights into the world of sleep, I had the privilege of engaging in a captivating conversation with Allison Brager, PhD.

Dr. Allison is a distinguished neurobiologist renowned for her expertise in sleep and circadian rhythms. As a major in the United States Army, her pioneering research examines the intricate domains of sleep, sleep deprivation, and the impact of stress on our minds and bodies. Her remarkable contributions extend to the world of literature, with her book *Meathead: Unraveling the Athletic Brain*, offering an intriguing exploration of the human brain's role in athletic performance.

So let's delve into the fascinating realm of sleep with Dr. Allison. This conversation promises to illuminate the mysteries of sleep, unveil its critical role in our lives, and reveal the keys to achieving restful nights and vibrant days.

Q: What is important for us to know about you?

---

[25] Centers for Disease Control and Prevention (CDC), "Long Work Hours and Shift Work Disorders," accessed February 7, 2024, www.cdc.gov/niosh/work-hour-training-for-nurses/longhours/mod3/08.html.

I practice what I preach. I've been an athlete my whole life and competed professionally in CrossFit. I was a collegiate athlete, so I always understood sleep as important. Even though the military does not make getting sleep easy sometimes, I knew it was important. To this day, I still am a good advocate for healthy sleep habits in the military.

Q: You're a neurobiologist? What is that?

I study the inner workings of the brain from a cellular level and how certain genetic factors change brain circuits. Then I look at what impact that has on behavior or how certain behaviors, such as destructive behaviors, have on the cell. It's like a genes to brain to behavior approach, but then also a behavior to brain to genes approach.

Q: You say you practice what you preach. Was there ever a time when you didn't think sleep was important and you learned from that? If so, why did sleep become so important?

I have always known sleep is important. I believe healthy sleep habits start with your parents. I was raised in a lower-middle-class, blue-collar family in Ohio. I'm actually one of the first people in my family to go to college. Despite my parents not making a lot of money, they had a very structured schedule and always made sure I got a good night's sleep.

Q: I was reading the article you wrote in *Medium* where you shared that sleep is really like a bank account. Could you explain what you meant by this?

Sleep really is like a bank account to put hours into. For every poor night of sleep, it takes about two nights of good sleep to make up for it.

Q: No! I didn't know that! I can understand this, though, because I work with a lot of older adults, and many express frustrations because it's almost impossible for them to get a good night's sleep. One of the biggest concerns they have is getting up to go to the bathroom. Is that biological or what?

Unfortunately, with aging, everything related to sleep declines as well. That's why it becomes essential to practice good sleep habits. This means having a structured bedtime where you're going to bed at the same time every night, you're dimming the lights, you're putting away your phone, all those things. Little things contribute to a really good night of sleep.

Q: I've recommended that people get the TV out of their bedroom, and they just laugh. Many of them share that it's the only way they can fall asleep, and it isn't until they wake up in the middle of the night that they will turn off the lights and go back to sleep. Is that disrupting a healthy sleep pattern?

Absolutely! When you're in dim light, you secrete melatonin, a hormone that is released and tells your body to prepare for sleep. Yet the biggest disrupter to melatonin is technology. Consequently, people who sleep with the television on might be able to get to sleep because they are tired, but the quality of their sleep is diminished.

Q: And what do you think about blue light blocking glasses?

Those are great. There's a lot of evidence to show they help maximize melatonin release at night. The issue I still have about them is that they give people an excuse to do something stimulating and excite the brain that they wouldn't otherwise do. Part of preparing for sleep is to start relaxing at least an hour and a half before going to bed. Do not do anything stimulating. Sleep should be a gradual transition.

We don't go from a state of being awake to deep sleep very quickly. There are stages. It's a gradual process where we hit stage one and stage two sleep, which are super light. And then from there, we go into stage three sleep, which is the deep restorative sleep that really chips away at our sleep debt. That whole process can take anywhere from sixty to ninety minutes before we actually hit that deep stage of sleep.

One way to coax and speed up that process of getting to deep sleep quicker is by relaxing our brains earlier in the evening.

Q: What suggestions do you have for that?

The big thing is to stop working at least ninety minutes before bed and put away your cell phone and turn off the TV sixty minutes before bed. Use a dim light, whether it's for reading a book or working on a puzzle. Also, taking a shower to help cool down your body and then getting into bed that is in a dark, cool, and quiet room. So that's where the structured routine comes in.

Q: When you say cool room, what temperature should it be?

Optimal temperature is between sixty-six and sixty-eight degrees. I know that's hard for a lot of people to consider. I have a cooling pad called Chilipad by ChiliSleep [available at https://sleep.me/product/cube-sleep-system]. It's an investment at first, but worth it. It helps keep you cool at night, and a lot of people report having better sleep quality from it.

Q: Are these cooling pads effective for women during menopause?

Absolutely. Menopause is the most disruptive to sleep—more so than any other time in adult life. These cooling pads may be very helpful for a woman who is going through menopause or when you have hot flashes, sweating, and fluctuations in your body temperature.

Q: What technologies do you think are helpful for a person to sleep?

Sleep trackers are good for doing baseline sleep assessments on yourself and then figuring out how your behavior changes sleep patterns. Fitness trackers are good for showing how disruptive exercise—exercise that is done close to bedtime—can be. Some common sleep trackers include Oura Ring [https://ouraring.com], WHOOP [https://www.whoop.com/us/en], and various smartwatches.

Q: Could technology help us understand how our lifestyle behaviors during the daytime impact our sleep?

By watching our daytime activities and behaviors, such as diet and exercise, these trackers offer valuable insights into how our lifestyle choices affect sleep quality. For example, they can help users recognize patterns linking an unhealthy diet to poor sleep or show correlations between exercise levels and sleep quality. Overall, they are good for providing behavioral awareness. The one thing I will say about sleep trackers, though, is that they are not clinical-grade devices. There's no sleep tracker out there today that is as good as going to a sleep clinic to get a sleep study done. So the data from the trackers has to be interpreted with caution.

Q: Have you found that most people are aware of the importance of sleep?

QUALITY SLEEP: TIME TO RECHARGE YOUR CELLS

For the most part, people are aware of the importance of sleep, yet there seems to be an invincibility complex. People think to themselves, Well, I'm the exception. I don't need seven to nine hours of sleep. The truth is that only zero point zero one percent of the population are exceptions. We all think that sleep is everyone else's problem, not our own problem. Ignorance is bliss. I think that's why a lot of people are unwilling to invest in sleep trackers because they truly don't want to know how terrible their sleep is.

Q: What does the research say about alcohol consumption and its impact on sleep?

Actually, that's what I've studied most of my career—twenty years. My PhD dissertation was on the direct impact of alcohol and cocaine on sleep. Anything past two drinks will disrupt your sleep—especially if you're drinking at night. We found that, as it relates to a good night's sleep, if you are going to drink at all, the best time of day to drink is in the middle of the afternoon. This way, the alcohol is metabolized by the time you go to bed.

Q: Why does alcohol have such a negative impact on sleep?

When we are sleeping with an excessive amount of alcohol in our system, we might fall asleep quickly, but then as soon as that alcohol is metabolized by the liver, there's an immediate, compensatory response. The body and brain experience insomnia because it's been overloaded with inhibitory signals for the last few hours. The result is that the brain gets excited.

When it comes to sleep deprivation, it's a vicious cycle, right? You know . . . we're sleep-deprived, we can't sleep, we have issues falling asleep, so we take alcohol, that in turn disrupts our sleep, which keeps making the problem worse and worse instead of better.

Q: That's fascinating—I had no idea that the alcohol causes our brain to get overloaded with inhibitory signals, which wake us up, creating insomnia.

Yeah, alcohol is very disruptive to sleep. It's more disruptive than people think. It prevents you from getting restorative sleep. I think people realize it once they have a sleep tracker, and then they may reduce their alcohol consumption because of what they learned.

Q: How much time should you allow between your last drink and sleep?

About three hours before bedtime. This is also true for food. Ideally, you want to go to bed in a fasting state. The reason is because your blood sugar levels won't be high, which will help you stay asleep. You don't want to eat too close to bedtime. And if you do have to eat, choose foods with very little sugar or fat.

Q: When it comes to the value of sleep, what is something people really don't recognize or appreciate?

Falling asleep is a process. It's not that your head hits the pillow and you're at once asleep. If that's happening, it means you're severely sleep-deprived, or you have a sleep disorder. As I shared earlier, the act of falling asleep should begin at least sixty to ninety minutes before bed. Overall, people do not respect or appreciate the time and investment you have to make to get a good night's sleep.

Q: Very true. It wasn't until my midthirties that I discovered that a good night's sleep was essential for my health and well-being.

I had a lot of stress, and like many people, I was juggling work, family, and other responsibilities. It was so bad that my symptoms resembled multiple sclerosis. Since that time, I have been what I refer to as "sleep sensitive." Is it unusual to be so sleep sensitive?

It actually is very common. After periods of extreme stress, a little bit of sleep deprivation is going to have an exacerbating response. I'm in the military and have been an athlete my whole life. I've had my handful of concussions. I'm very sensitive to sleep deprivation now because of concussions. Yet I didn't know there was a link between concussions and sleep until I started studying it when I was at Walter Reed [National Military Medical Center]. Now there is more information coming out on concussions and the issue of being very sleep sensitive. What it means is that if you're in a similar situation, you really have to set up a routine to perfect your sleep.

Q: I really believe that many people resign themselves to a life of sleep deprivation or maybe give up on the thought that they can improve the quality of their sleep. How does sleep deprivation impact us on a cellular level?

Sleep's important because that's really when the restoration and recovery of cells happens. During sleep, anabolic hormones are released, which are absolutely necessary to repair tissue. Additionally, sleep is also necessary to clear toxic waste and free radicals that build up in our brain.

There are three hormones in general that are also impacted: testosterone, human growth hormone, and insulin growth factor. The release of these hormones only happens during the deepest stage of non-REM sleep. It's called slow-wave sleep. If you don't have slow-wave sleep because of a sleep disorder or poor sleep quality due to poor sleep habits, then you never get that recovery response. That hormone release trickles down to a cellular level, so you accumulate free radicals, which you do not want. The disruption of these growth factors is called neurotrophic growth factors, and brain-derived neurotrophic factor, BDNF, is a big one. When you lose the ability to produce BDNF, it disrupts part of the recovery process and preservation of brain health. Again, inflammatory factors that build up, even at the level of mitochondria in the cell, they're not going to get the replenishment of ATP as quickly. ATP is the source of energy for use and storage at the cellular level, which is really important. Consequently, instead of building up ATP, they're using it because the brain and body are still active. It is a whole cascade of events.

Q: The idea of slow-wave sleep is fascinating. Do you mean that someone could be in bed for six or even nine hours, but if they don't get into that state of slow-wave sleep, they will lose out on some of the real benefits of sleep and the repair of the cells?

It's better to get four hours of deep sleep than it is to get nine hours of poor sleep. Many studies have revealed that subjects who sleep deeply for four hours actually perform better than people who sleep terribly for nine hours.

Q: So, getting to bed earlier is one of your top recommendations. But where does the idea of circadian rhythms fit in? Aren't we all different? I know many people who believe they are night owls. Is this not true? Or are we really programmed from an evolutionary perspective to go to sleep when the sun goes down and wake up when the sun comes up?

Based on the research, eighty percent of the world should go to bed after sunset and rise with sunrise. Ten percent are genetic night owls. I'm one of those people. My parents were night owls too. It is something that's inherited through family genetics. That leaves ten percent of the population who are true morning people.

Yet I believe society has shifted us to become morning people. The military tries to make me a morning person, yet I fight back against it.

Q: Is this where technology can be beneficial because while we sleep, we are only minimally aware of the quality of our sleep?

Sleep is an unconscious state, and you're only aware of it when you wake up in the morning. If you don't feel well rested or rejuvenated, you probably didn't get deep sleep. Technology can provide valuable information—however, it is not an exact science. If someone has sleep challenges, they need to see their doctor, who will decide whether or not they need a comprehensive sleep study to objectively discover what is happening during their sleep.

Q: How does everything we're discussing translate into having energy during the day?

Dr. William Dement, the godfather of sleep medicine, used to say, "Sleepiness makes you stupid." And it's really true. You become so detached from reality, and a lower level of performance becomes your new reality.

The number one diagnostic or symptom of chronic sleep deprivation is daytime sleepiness. If you're someone who wants to fall asleep during the day, you have an issue. Even if you are doing highly engaging active work during the day but you want to fall asleep, you have an issue.

Or if you have a workout routine but are struggling to keep your intensity, whether it's strength or stamina, well, that may be a sign of inability to recover from insufficient sleep.

Q: As an athlete with a very demanding job, how are you able to balance everything? How do you have the time?

I prioritize my sleep and make sure I get eight to nine hours of sleep every night. This has even impacted my career choices. When I was younger, the husband of my gymnastics coach told me to select a career that catered to my lifestyle. I am glad I took his advice. Quite honestly, that's why I'll never take a high leadership position in the military. I don't have it in me to sacrifice my sleep for it. So, I'm happy being like a supporting element and staff.

Q: Now, as people get older and retire, how do you think all this fits in with sleep?

It's a challenge because with age, the quality of sleep does decline, especially around the time of menopause. It's very challenging for women.

Q: How about for men who are getting older. How does their sleep change?

Men have hormonal changes too, which include a decline in testosterone. Low levels of testosterone disrupt sleep; normal levels help promote sleep.

My advice is when you wake up in the middle of the night, do not turn on a light because it stops the release of melatonin, and your body thinks it is time to get up. If you must have some light, use a dim nightlight.

Q: What are the daytime effects when someone consistently lacks a good night's sleep, affecting their body's toxin removal and cell repair processes?

Those toxins continue to accumulate—it really amounts to a credit or debit system. So if you don't get good sleep, those toxins continue to accumulate. Initially, it might not lead to a clinical issue. Even weeks or months, the toxins may accumulate, but over the course of the year, they can lead to neurodegeneration and gastrointestinal ulcers. It can lead to the inability to lose weight.

Q: How does mental health impact sleep?

Your mental health has a direct impact on sleep. And as I mentioned earlier, increased stress affects the sympathetic nervous system, which is a huge driver of sleep quality. If your body is in a fearful state, it doesn't want to go to sleep. But if the stress is managed and good sleep hygiene skills are developed, sleep quality improves. And when sleep improves, the body can repair and restore itself on a cellular level. Unfortunately, when you have a bad night of sleep due to stress, you might get stressed about getting good sleep the next night, which results in you having another poor night's sleep. It can be a vicious cycle. And so, it's compounding stress. And it's just like an overall vicious cycle—not being able to manage your sleep is going to make you irritable. Sleep deprivation makes us irritable, volatile, and essentially, our emotional system becomes hijacked.

Q: If someone has been experiencing chronic sleep deprivation and now wants to make a change, how long can they expect it to take before they see improvements in their sleep quality and overall well-being?

It can happen right away. My friends are cognitive psychologists, and they will tell you it could take anywhere from a week to a few months. I would say that there's a continuum, but depending on the level of commitment you're willing to make, it could take up to two months.

Q: Are there studies about how breathwork impacts sleep?

Breathwork has a huge positive impact on sleep. It's because you are channeling and tapping into the parasympathetic nervous system, which is important for recovery. Medications are just a band-aid. Most medications prematurely and artificially treat the root of the problem. I vote for a lot of holistic health practices that don't involve medications to help with sleep.

Q: As an athlete, does fitness help improve sleep, or does sleep improve fitness?

It's both, yet there's a balance. When I was competing professionally, I always knew when I was on the brink of overtraining because my sleep would be awful. People who do a general, normal amount of fitness—not psychotic amounts like I used to do—will have better quality sleep because their body needs it.

Exercise is a natural compensatory response, and by also getting that good night's sleep, they have built up the reserves and the ability to continue to do that exercise.

Q: Earlier, you said we should not exercise right before going to bed. What research has been done on this?

It depends on the type of exercise. There is conflicting evidence—much of the research that exists does not look at high-intensity exercise. They're basically looking at populations of people who are walking. If you're taking a brisk walk or doing something that doesn't jack up your heart rate, you could do that pretty much all the way up till bedtime. But if you're going into your home gym or taking a bootcamp or a CrossFit workout, you're not going to sleep for a few hours after doing that because you just turned on that sympathetic nervous system.

Q: How does food impact sleep?

The quality of your food matters. There are even sleep-promoting foods, and none of these are processed. They include walnuts, dates, kiwis, and cherries to help promote sleep. Foods you need to avoid are processed foods and foods high in fat and sugar. Again, it goes back to avoiding elevating blood sugar levels.

Q: What would be your top five recommendations to improve sleep?

One, create a sleep schedule that works for you, which includes finding things to do at least sixty minutes before bed that promote good sleep—things that don't involve your phone or TV.

Two, use dim light to stimulate natural melatonin release.

Three, go to bed earlier. Benjamin Franklin used to say, "Early to bed, early to rise, makes a man happy, healthy, and wise." There's some truth to that, because if you go to bed early, you're setting yourself up for success to get better sleep.

Four, don't have a TV or technology in your bedroom.

Five, if you have a dog or a partner who's very disruptive to your sleep, sleep in another room so your sleep isn't disrupted.

America really is one of the few countries in the world where we co-sleep. Many Europeans and Asians have really good sleep health, and they sleep in separate bedrooms. So don't take it as an insult when your partner wants to get a better night's sleep because he or she finds there's something about the way you sleep that disrupts their sleep.

Unlocking the Science of Sleep: Insights and Strategies from Allison Brager, PhD

Let's review the key points from Dr. Brager's interview:

Importance of Prioritizing Sleep

Dr. Allison emphasizes the crucial role sleep plays in overall health and well-being. She practices what she preaches and ensures she gets eight to nine hours of sleep every night, even if it means making career choices that align with her sleep needs.

Neurobiology and Behavior

She explains her work as a neurobiologist, studying the brain from a cellular level and how genetics, brain circuits, and behavior interact. This holistic approach helps us understand how sleep impacts behavior and vice versa.

Sleep as a Process

Falling asleep is not an instant process. Dr. Allison highlights that it should begin sixty to ninety minutes before bedtime, involving a gradual transition to deep sleep stages.

Tips for Improving Your Sleep Environment

Dimming lights, avoiding technology before bed, keeping a cool room temperature, and setting up a structured bedtime routine.

Impact of Alcohol

Alcohol can disrupt sleep patterns, especially when consumed close to bedtime. It prevents the body from entering deep sleep and can negatively impact your sleep quality.

Effects of Aging on Sleep

Aging often leads to declining sleep quality. She suggested strategies like keeping a structured bedtime and using dim night lights for those who often wake up in the middle of the night.

Exercise and Sleep

There is a relationship between exercise and sleep. Dr. Allison emphasized the importance of understanding the type and timing of exercise to avoid disrupting sleep patterns.

Diet and Sleep

Certain foods can promote sleep, such as walnuts, dates, kiwis, and cherries. Conversely, processed foods high in fat and sugar can negatively affect sleep.

Please see the Acknowledgments and Contact Information section at the end of the book for more details about Dr. Brager.

A Vibrant Sage Must Sleep for a Vibrant Life!

As we complete this chapter on the fourth pillar of vibrant living, it's essential to pause and reflect on the significance of sleep in our lives. It's easy to underestimate the power of a good night's rest, but remember these words: "Each day is a gift, and to be my best for myself and others, I have to sleep."

Why is sleep so important for you?

What does your bedtime routine look like? Does it support your overall well-being?

As you contemplate these questions, I'll leave you with a final set of thoughts and practical steps to enhance your sleep, your health, and your life:

1. **Harness the Power of Breath:** Your breath is a friend that can help calm your mind, especially on nights when racing

thoughts and anxiety threaten to keep you awake. Practice deep breathing exercises to prepare your body for relaxation.
2. **Create a Healthy Sleep Routine:** Create a pre-sleep routine that disconnects you from technology at least two hours before bedtime. Substitute screen time with activities like reading, listening to soothing music or podcasts, meditating, being intimate, or taking a relaxing bath or shower.
3. **Minimize Bedroom Distractions:** Keep technology away from your sleeping area and reduce, or better yet, eliminate sources of light and high electromagnetic fields (EMF).
4. **Maintain a Cool Sleeping Environment:** Ensure that your bedroom is comfortably cool, as a cooler room can promote better sleep.
5. **Mindful Eating:** Avoid eating heavy meals or snacks within three hours of bedtime to help both your brain and digestive system.
6. **Calm Your Mind:** Refrain from engaging with stressful content like news, social media, or intense movies in the hours leading up to sleep.
7. **Bedtime Rituals:** Develop bedtime rituals that you genuinely enjoy, such as sipping herbal tea (but avoid it too close to bedtime), journaling to clear your mind, or using aromatherapy with calming essential oils like lavender.
8. **Embrace the Morning:** Upon waking, take a deep breath and relish the gift of a new day. Starting the day with gratitude can set a positive tone.
9. **Moderate Alcohol Consumption:** Limit alcohol intake and avoid drinking it too close to bedtime, as it can negatively impact sleep quality. Ideally, stop drinking within three hours of bedtime.

10. **Cherish Intimacy:** Recognize the benefits of intimacy, not only for enhancing sleep but also for energizing your body, mind, and soul.

Sleep is not merely a period of rest; it's a crucial phase of cellular repair, detoxification, and mental rejuvenation. We explored how sleep is intricately linked to circadian rhythms, hormonal balance, and the elimination of waste from our bodies. Additionally, we discovered how sleep directly influences heart health, immunity, and even our intimate relationships.

With the importance of sleep firmly proven, we're now ready to move on to the final pillar of our journey: discovering the significance of purpose in living a vibrant and passionate life. Stay tuned for the grand finale!

Before you turn the page to the next chapter of your life, I encourage you to take a moment of introspection. Be honest about your sleep habits and ask yourself, *why do you value sleep, and how does your bedtime routine align with your overall well-being?*

CHAPTER 8

PILLAR FIVE

PURPOSE-DRIVEN HEALTH: THE SECRET TO A VIBRANT LIFE

No, this is not the beginning of a new chapter in my life; this is the beginning of a new book! That first book is already closed, ended, and tossed into the seas; this new book is newly opened, has just begun!
— C. Joybell C.

Life gifts us wisdom as we navigate its diverse landscapes. Your treasure trove of experiences has shaped you into the remarkable person you are today.

Living with purpose is the thread that weaves through every pillar in the framework of vibrant aging—a thread that's been part of your life's tapestry for decades. It's about sharing your unique gifts with the world, embracing joy, love, serenity, and contentment, and perfecting your health regardless of your age or life's twists and turns.

When I began writing this book, I knew purpose had to be my fifth and final pillar. But why, you may ask? Because purpose isn't just another ingredient in the recipe for a vibrant life—it's the secret sauce that infuses every aspect of your existence with meaning and vitality. It's the light that shines brightest when you face challenges or moments when motivation wanes. You may not need scientific studies to confirm this truth, for you've felt it deep within your heart, perhaps through your own experiences or watching loved ones.

As we explore how purpose can illuminate your path and enhance your health, remember that each chapter of life offers fresh opportunities to align with a purpose that transcends societal norms and personal ambitions. Your journey to becoming a vibrant sage is a testament to the enduring power of purpose in aging gracefully.

How has your sense of purpose evolved over the course of your life?

Growing up, I never consciously pondered the question, What is my purpose in life? However, I carried within me an innate desire to make a difference, to help others—a calling that brought me joy and anticipation. This desire found different expressions in various stages of my life.

During my formative years, my sense of purpose was revealed through community engagement. I took on roles such as organizing events in my beloved 4-H club and playing in the fire department's band. I eagerly embraced opportunities to contribute to both my local community and the world at large. One cherished memory stands out: creating a lifesaver candy man with a resident at a nearby nursing home. It makes me wonder if acts of humanitarianism enrich the hearts of both parties.

College introduced me to new possibilities and ignited my curiosity about the world. It was a time of exploration, where the pursuit of knowledge in liberal arts and the sciences laid the foundation for my future path. Throughout my undergraduate and graduate studies, I had numerous opportunities to craft my professional skills by working in schools, hospitals, and residential facilities. These experiences provided opportunities to work with individuals across the age spectrum and with various communication challenges. Each was a priceless learning experience and strengthened my inherent drive to help others. Furthermore, it stirred a sense of potential, a realization that there was more to life than meets the eye.

Fast-forward to graduation, and a new chapter unfolded. Family and work became my immediate and all-encompassing purposes for the next two decades. It was a demanding but fulfilling phase of my life, where every day was dedicated to nurturing and providing for my loved ones and my clients. The joy and satisfaction that came from these roles were undeniable, yet beneath the surface, I could feel something evolving.

As my children grew and became more independent and my job situations evolved, I found myself at a crossroads, where the roles that had defined my purpose for so long began to shift. The dynamics of my family life changed as my children pursued their own paths, and my career went through transformations. It was a period of profound change that brought both challenges and opportunities.

This transition prompted deep self-reflection and a reevaluation of what purpose meant to me at this stage of life. It was a reminder that purpose is not static; it evolves with us. It's a journey within the journey, a story within the story.

I realized that while family and work had been my driving forces, they were not the entirety of my purpose. Instead, they were chapters in a larger narrative. The desire to make a meaningful difference in the lives of others, which had always been present, began to take on a new form. My sense of purpose expanded beyond immediate responsibilities to encompass a broader view of how I could contribute to the world around me.

This shift in perspective became a pivotal moment that allowed me to embrace the changing seasons of life with renewed purpose. It reinforced the idea that living with purpose is not a one-size-fits-all concept; rather, it evolves and adapts as we journey through life's diverse landscapes.

I believe that without that shift, you would not be reading this book, and I would not be sharing my insatiable desire to empower others on their journey toward vibrant aging. It's a journey we're embarking on together, filled with the wisdom of evolving purpose.

Now, I invite you to pause and reflect on the moments in your life that have kindled a sense of purpose. *Have you ever stood at a crossroads, torn between societal expectations and your own dreams?* Think back to your teen years and early twenties. *Did external pressures influence the trajectory of your life and lead you down a path you hadn't initially envisioned?*

Life presents unexpected twists and turns. There are moments when we must set aside our dreams and ambitions to embrace responsibilities such as starting a family, moving away from home, or pursuing a career. It's in these moments that our sense of purpose may seem to fade into the background. But, my dear friends, it's essential to remember that purpose evolves, just as life does.

Consider this scenario: Meet Eileen a young woman who once envisioned herself as an entrepreneur. However, life took an unexpected turn when she became a mother. While motherhood brought her immeasurable joy, she couldn't ignore the yearning for something more—a sense that her life's purpose remained unfulfilled. Eileen revisited her childhood dream of entrepreneurship and found renewed purpose through creating scented stuffed animals that soothed children. Her son enthusiastically joined in, and soon, her small business thrived. *This stands as a testament to the power of reconnecting with one's calling.*

Eileen's pursuit of purpose not only brought her fulfillment, but it also rekindled the spark of life within her. *Can you recall a moment in your life when unexpected circumstances led you to rediscover your true purpose?* The transformative power of purpose is clear—it has the potential to enrich our lives and reignite our passion for life itself.

Embracing Life's Unpredictability: Finding Purpose in Every Challenge

Life's challenges and transitions offer a unique opportunity to realign with our purpose. Whether you've followed a path that's closely aligned with your innate sense of purpose or you've navigated through life meeting society's expectations and financial demands, every phase of life offers a chance to reevaluate and take intentional steps forward. As a vibrant sage—regardless of your age or where you currently stand in life—it's essential to recognize that as we get older, we face unique challenges. These obstacles may make us question whether the struggle is worth it, whether it's worth continuing to move forward. But the answer, my friend, is a resounding YES!

It's in these times of adversity and negative emotions that the seeds of transformation are sown. I believe we can all identify with moments when life veered unexpectedly. My personal odyssey in recognizing the significance of embracing and discovering purpose within life's challenges began during the COVID-19 lockdown—a period when countless individuals, if not the entire world, felt disconnected and helpless.

In the first days of the pandemic, I sought solace in creating online videos dedicated to helping others with their health and wellness. Although these videos served as a lifeline, I felt a lingering sense of melancholy. The awareness that I had not reached a sufficient number of people, particularly those most susceptible to the virus, weighed heavily on my heart.

Amid the trials of this tumultuous period, my father's health took a severe downturn, ultimately leading to his passing. His departure added layers of sorrow to an already challenging time. A few months after his passing, an undeniable compulsion overcame me—to write. Uncertain of what form these words would take, I began to pour my knowledge, experiences, and emotions onto paper, thus laying the foundation for this book. It was a journey of rediscovery, a rekindling of my life's purpose.

When I speak of rekindling my life's purpose, I'm alluding to a profound connection that I unearthed deep within my heart and cells. It was a purpose that moved me to tears—an overflowing wellspring of love, connection, and authenticity. Writing this book became not only a vehicle but a lifeline, offering me an avenue to reignite my sense of purpose. The struggles, challenges, and hardships I experienced had transformed into stepping stones, guiding me toward a greater sense of meaning.

Throughout my life, my work was never just a job; it was a passion and a source of profound joy. Helping and supporting others to conquer their challenges filled my heart with happiness. My life was enriched by the dreams and aspirations of each client and every individual I had the privilege to work with.

Now, I'd like to turn the spotlight on you: *What does living a purposeful life mean to you? How has your belief about how your life should be lived evolved over the years? Are you currently aligned with your sense of purpose?* It's possible that you've experienced moments when life temporarily steered you away from your heart's mission and purpose. But remember, reflecting on your life's purpose is like a beacon that can rescue you and set you back on track.

Life is a tapestry woven with twists and turns, highs and lows, each offering a unique opportunity to rediscover and realign with our purpose.

Four months after my father's passing, an uncharted chapter in my life's story began. It all started with the simple act of journaling my emotions, frustrations, and sense of helplessness and putting my accumulated knowledge and experiences onto paper. At the time, I held only a faint hope that these scattered thoughts would someday coalesce into this very book. Little did I know that this process would become my lifeline—a way to rediscover life with a newfound purpose.

In the following months, I gradually realized the significance of embracing the course of my entire life, both the smooth sailing and, possibly even more importantly, the challenging and turbulent moments. It became clear that these struggles, challenges, and hardships were the very catalysts for my personal growth and transformation.

Possible Interconnection of Purpose and Health

Early in my career, the seeds of a profound question had taken root in my mind: Is there a deep connection between one's sense of purpose and one's health? As a speech pathologist, I've always been fascinated by the intricate interplay between an individual's purpose and their overall well-being.

Throughout my career, I met countless clients who underwent significant health challenges, often coinciding with their retirement. What struck me was the remarkable pattern that appeared—many of them faced unexpected health challenges, such as strokes, during these transitional phases. This recurring observation intensified my curiosity. I couldn't help but ponder whether there might be a correlation between losing one's life's purpose, which is not that uncommon after retirement, and the heightened vulnerability to such health setbacks.

This question has lingered in my thoughts, an unspoken curiosity that longed for answers. It's a question that touches on the very essence of our existence and how it evolves over time. And as you'll soon discover, scientific research offers compelling insights into the connection between living life with purpose and our physical and mental well-being. But before we delve into the science behind this intricate relationship and its profound implications for health outcomes, I want to share a deeply personal and inspiring story about my father.

Have you ever wondered if your sense of purpose is intricately tied to your health and vitality?

Have you ever seen someone navigate a life-altering change and emerge from it with grace and a renewed sense of purpose?

Having higher purpose provides individuals with a greater will to live, and this enables people to bear more short-term discomfort since they can appreciate why discomfort is worth enduring.
— Viktor Frankl's Key Theory

My Father's Remarkable Life Guided by Purpose

As I reflect on my life, I can clearly see how profoundly my father, Henry T. Waring, influenced it. He was not just a father; he was an inspirational presence—a vibrant sage who lived an extraordinary life filled with purpose, connection, courage, and strength, despite facing many challenges. His legacy continues to cast its guiding light on my path and is an enduring reminder that purpose can be revealed even in the midst of adversity. Please allow me to give you a glimpse into his remarkable journey and share one of the most valuable lessons he ever taught me: Embrace a life of purpose.

Dad was born in Deerfield, Illinois, in 1922. He was a child of the Depression, and due to financial struggles, his family was forced to move to Chaptico, Maryland, a very small town in Southern Maryland, to live with extended family. Ten years later, he enlisted in the navy. Dad's early life was not easy, but he had a loving family and a strong community supporting him. As an adult, Dad lived by many of the values he saw as a child—he gave generously, both time and resources, to his family, business, and community.

Dad worked hard to support his family, and while I don't believe he was conscious of his lifestyle habits, he was very active. He loved playing tennis and golf. Given all the farms in the community, he ate an overall healthy diet of locally sourced vegetables, fruits, fish, and meats. Now, he wasn't perfect—he loved his ice cream and chocolate.

Despite living a generally healthy lifestyle and rarely needing a doctor, that changed in his early seventies. Within the span of less than two years, he had both hips replaced and underwent quadruple bypass surgery. This was not uncommon for someone his age. Yet the defining period in his life was when he was diagnosed with prostate cancer and given only two years to live.

I cannot even begin to guess all the emotions that churned up inside him when he was given that death sentence, but one thing was for sure: he was not ready to die. He had dreams to fulfill and too much to live for—family, friends, employees, and his community. Possibly there were even some regrets he needed to rectify. Because of his strength of purpose combined with excellent medical care, both traditional and unconventional, he made a full recovery from cancer and lived another 28 years.

Dad lived with an open and generous heart. He lived with purpose! Whether a stranger or close friend, Dad loved connecting with others. Dad was a philanthropist. He was not like many of those today who have millions of dollars and use philanthropy to shield their money. Instead, he used his wealth to help others less fortunate—he gave generously to many nonprofit organizations, including those that cared for the homeless or women and children who had been abused. Education was also especially important to him—he believed strongly in the power of education. The lack of opportunities for many African Americans and immigrants in this country upset him. He supported programs and scholarships that provided educational opportunities at the local level, working closely both with churches and St. Mary's College in Southern Maryland.

As much as Dad gave to others, he was always extremely committed to his seven children and many grandchildren. Yet, following his cancer, it seemed like his love for each of us deepened. I believe this was the first time that family became number one in his life. My fondest memories are not from my childhood days but rather from the last thirty years of his life—trips to Europe, weekends in New York City, hanging out playing poker, discussing challenges, and seeking advice. Dad was there for each of us with an open heart, and, most importantly, he listened attentively to us.

Between the ages of seventy and ninety, Dad showed more vitality than ever before in his life. He exemplified the essence of vibrant aging, embodying what it truly means to be a vibrant sage.

Embracing both the physical and emotional changes that come with age, he continued to lead a fulfilling life.

But then he lost his sight. Losing one's vision means losing one's independence. In many ways, this may have been more challenging than his cancer.

For many, a sudden loss of vision, especially when you're ninety, may have slowed a person down, but not Dad. The adjustment was difficult, but it didn't stop him from serving his community and being a supportive, loving father. One of Dad's greatest pleasures during his last eight years was helping others through simple acts of kindness. He took his grandchildren to music and art classes (his live-in companion did the driving). Dad enjoyed weekly lunches with friends and business partners. One of his sweetest acts of kindness was that he would buy at least ten dozen eggs and bags of fresh produce from the Amish so he could share the food with others. He was focused on little acts of kindness, and when he gave to others, he was so happy.

My dad died on November 7, 2020, at the age of ninety-eight, just twenty-two months shy of his one-hundredth birthday. He had hoped to reach triple digits, but that was not meant to be. At that time, the world was changing around him due to the pandemic, which had a profound impact on all our lives, including my father's. It isolated him from family, friends, and the activities he lived for. I honestly believe he would have lived to be one hundred if his life had continued with purpose, love, and family.

Life takes on a deeper meaning when lived with purpose—an inner compass that not only guides our actions but also shapes our physical and emotional well-being. Vibrant aging is centered around living life with a heart-driven purpose! It is only possible when you come from a place in your heart that is greater than yourself.

My father was a man who loved life and who deeply cared about his family, friends, and community. Yet I believe his cancer prognosis inspired him to embrace life in a way he had never done before. He became more purposeful. He gained courage and tenacity. With all my heart, I believe he regained his health because he loved other people, especially his family. He was passionate about leaving this earth a better place than when he was born.

Unlocking the Secrets of Purpose: From Ancient Wisdom to Modern Science

Thoughts and emotions have a significant impact on our gene expression as well as our body's inflammatory response.
— BRUCE LIPTON, PhD, CELLULAR BIOLOGIST

As I explored whether purpose and health are intertwined, I found myself connecting the dots between my intuitive hunch and the enduring wisdom treasured by ancient cultures and across different traditions, from the Eastern philosophy of dharma to the Greek concept of eudemonia. Eudemonic happiness is about individual happiness based on a sense of purpose . . . to have meaning in life. The recurring theme throughout the ages appears to be that a sense of purpose is not just a philosophical ideal but a key ingredient for a fulfilling life. It's a belief that has transcended generations and cultures, standing the test of time.

Even more intriguing is that modern science has added empirical evidence to this ageless wisdom. Researchers have unveiled a compelling narrative that suggests purpose-driven living influences not only our mental and emotional well-being, but it also extends its reach to our physical health and even our genes.

At some level, this almost seems like common sense—of course, when we live a life with purpose, we're healthier—but the question is why. Given that we are living longer, science is exploring whether something as simple yet profound as having a purpose could be a tool or a way to improve not just lifespan but health span.

Within the scientific community, there is research specifically related to "Purpose in Life" (PiL). As the National Institute of Health aptly puts it, Purpose in Life (PIL) is a research area that focuses on the interaction between mind and body and the powerful ways in which emotional, mental, social, and spiritual factors can directly affect health.[26] It encompasses the idea that individuals can find purpose and fulfillment in various aspects of life, such as relationships, work, hobbies, or contributions to society. This concept recognizes that purpose may evolve and change over time as individuals grow and learn.

So, how does leading a life with purpose impact health and longevity? While earlier chapters explored well-researched areas like fitness, sleep, breath, and nutrition, this chapter addresses the more abstract yet crucial question of how purpose fits into the vibrant aging puzzle.

In this section, we'll examine four intriguing facets of how living with purpose can shape our well-being:

1. **Better Sleep When Living with Purpose:** Recent research illuminates the intricate connection between PiL and sleep quality. But it raises a captivating question: Does a profound sense of purpose lead to the gift of a good night's sleep, or does restful slumber pave the way for a life filled with purpose?

---

[26] Shian-Ling Keng, Moria J. Smoski, and Christopher J. Robins, "Effects of Mindfulness on Psychological Health: A Review of Empirical Studies," *Clinical Psychology Review* 31, no. 6 (August 2011): 1041–1056, doi:10.1016/j.cpr.2011.04.006, accessed January 7, 2024, https://www.ncbi.nlm.nih.gov/pmc/articles/PMC3679190.

2. **Cognition and Protecting the Brain:** We'll explore how nurturing your sense of purpose can potentially preserve and enhance cognitive function while offering fresh perspectives on a brighter and more fulfilling future.
3. **Link between PiL and Living Longer:** We'll uncover how a strong sense of purpose may not only reduce chronic lifestyle disorders but also directly affect lifespan, defy conventional expectations, and offer the promise of a longer, healthier life.
4. **Impact of Chronic Stress:** Is there a possible link between PiL and combating the pervasive influence of stress on our well-being? Read on to find out.

The Dreamy Effects of Living with Purpose

Imagine waking up after a night of deep, restorative sleep, feeling rejuvenated and ready to embrace the day ahead. Now, imagine that this peaceful slumber isn't just a result of your bedtime routine but is also influenced by your sense of purpose in life (PiL).

In 2017, a groundbreaking study conducted by Northwestern Medicine and Rush University Medical Center marked the first-ever exploration of the link between PiL and sleep. The findings unveiled a remarkable association between having a sense of purpose and improved sleep quality, along with fewer sleep disturbances, like sleep apnea and restless leg syndrome.

This study, centered around older adults, not only affirmed the general correlation between PiL and better sleep but also delved into the specific long-term benefits. A total of 823 non-demented participants, aged sixty to one hundred (with an average age of seventy-nine), participated. Those who reported having a sense of purpose were 63 percent less likely to experience sleep apnea and 52 percent less likely to suffer from restless leg syndrome.

Additionally, they reported moderately enhanced overall sleep quality.[27]

The research suggests that nurturing a sense of purpose in life might serve as a drug-free strategy to elevate the quality of one's sleep. Furthermore, the study hints at the potential effectiveness of mindfulness-based therapies in targeting PiL and harnessing their positive influence on sleep quality.

Protecting Your Mind: The Power of Purpose

Picture this: you're in your golden years, still mentally sharp, and your memory is as reliable as ever. You effortlessly tackle crossword puzzles, engage in stimulating conversations, and enjoy the thrill of learning new skills. Now, imagine that your secret weapon for preserving this cognitive vitality isn't a magic potion or a fountain of youth—it's your sense of purpose in life (PiL).

Research has unveiled intriguing connections between PiL and cognitive health. Middle-aged individuals with higher PiL have shown an impressive ability to resist cognitive decline, particularly in terms of their thinking abilities.[28] This suggests that nurturing your sense of purpose could act as a shield, protecting your cognitive function even as you enter middle age.

Furthermore, individuals with a robust PiL seem to have specific brain connections that bolster their cognitive performance. This underscores the importance of cultivating a sense of purpose as a proactive strategy for maintaining cognitive well-being.

Here's what makes this discovery even more exciting: PiL isn't set in stone; it can be cultivated and strengthened through

---

27 Marla Paul, "Purpose in Life Results in Better Sleep," *Northwestern University News*, July 10, 2017, accessed February 7, 2024, https://news.northwestern.edu/stories/2017/july/purpose-in-life-results-better-sleep/.

28 Amy P. Wingo et al., "Purpose in Life Is a Robust Protective Factor of Reported Cognitive Decline among Late Middle-Aged Adults: The Emory Healthy Aging Study," *Journal of Affective Disorders* 263, no. 2 (February 15, 2020): 310–317, doi:10.1016/j.jad.2019.11.124, accessed February 7, 2024, https://pubmed.ncbi.nlm.nih.gov/31969260.

interventions such as psychological therapies. This means that actively enhancing your sense of purpose could be a protective measure for your cognitive health as you age.

Intriguingly, extensive studies have uncovered patterns showing that people's sense of purpose tends to diminish both before and during cognitive impairment, with a more pronounced decline once cognitive impairment sets in. This decline could be attributed to underlying brain changes associated with this condition.

These research findings emphasize the importance of sustaining a sense of purpose, especially when cognitive impairment becomes a factor. It suggests that nurturing your sense of purpose isn't just beneficial for your overall well-being but might also contribute to cognitive recovery.[29]

Researchers at the Rush Alzheimer's Disease Center go as far as suggesting that PiL could be "brain-preserving."[30] Their investigations revealed that individuals with a strong sense of purpose experienced slower rates of age-related cognitive decline.

In another extensive study involving over eleven thousand adults aged fifty and older, researchers explored whether having a sense of purpose could be a defense against cognitive decline in older adults. The results were striking: a robust sense of purpose was linked to better cognitive scores and acted as a protective shield against cognitive decline, especially in older individuals and specific racial/ethnic groups.[31]

---

29 Patricia A. Thomas, Hui Liu, and Debra Umberson, "Family Relationships and Well-Being," *Innovations in Aging* 1, no. 3 (November 11, 2017), accessed February 7, 2024, www.ncbi.nlm.nih.gov/pmc/articles/PMC5954612.
30 "Boost Your Brain Health," Rush, accessed February 7, 2024, www.rush.edu/news/boost-your-brain-health.
31 Giyeon Kim et al., "Purpose in Life Protects Against Cognitive Decline Among Older Adults," *American Journal of Geriatric Psychiatry* 27, no. 6 (June 2019), accessed February 7, 2024, www.pubmed.ncbi.nlm.nih.gov/30824327.

Collectively, these two studies point to the notion that PiL may play a crucial role in preserving what experts call "cognitive reserve." This suggests that individuals with greater cognitive resilience at baseline are better equipped to withstand brain challenges before showing neurological symptoms.

Unlocking the Potential of Purpose: A Shield against Mortality

Two years to live—that's what the doctors told my father. It was a sentence that hung heavy over our family, casting a long shadow of uncertainty. But what unfolded in the next twenty-seven years was nothing short of miraculous—a life that defied expectations and left us wondering: Was it his unwavering sense of purpose that made the difference?

In one remarkable study led by Koizumi and his team, the association between PiL and mortality took center stage. The results left researchers and health professionals alike in awe. It was revealed that a strong sense of purpose in life was not just a philosophical concept but a powerful force for longevity. Those individuals with a robust PiL experienced a staggering 72 percent lower rate of death from stroke, a 44 percent lower rate of death from cardiovascular disease, and an impressive 48 percent lower rate of death from any cause.[32] And here's the kicker—it wasn't a fleeting effect. These findings were seen after an average of thirteen years of follow-up, solidifying the notion that purpose-driven living can significantly extend one's lifespan.

A recent study led by Koichiro Shiba, assistant professor of epidemiology at the School of Public Health at Boston University, found that higher levels of purpose in life are associated with a reduced risk of mortality from any cause. The study revealed that

---

[32] Masayo Koizumi et al., "Effect of Having a Sense of Purpose in Life on the Risk of Death from Cardiovascular Diseases," *Journal of Epidemiology* 18, no. 5 (2008): 191–196, doi:10.2188/jea.je2007388, accessed February 7, 2024, www.pubmed.ncbi.nlm.nih.gov/18753736.

individuals reporting the highest sense of purpose had the lowest mortality risk (15.2 percent), compared to those with the lowest sense of purpose (36.5 percent).[33]

Harnessing Purpose to Conquer Stress and Unlock a Healthier, More Vibrant Life

Stress is an ever-present companion in life, affecting us all in various ways. While we may not be aware of the science behind exactly what is happening in our bodies, we all can acknowledge that long-term stress can cast a shadow over our physical and mental well-being. It's like driving a car through heavy traffic and steep hills day after day; eventually, it takes a toll on the engine. This concept is what experts call "allostatic load," the cumulative impact of stress on our body's internal machinery.

Our bodies work hard to adapt to and cope with ongoing stressors, such as work pressures, financial concerns, or personal challenges. Yet when stress becomes chronic, it can lead to wear and tear on our physiological systems, potentially causing health issues like heart disease, diabetes, and even mental health struggles. But here's where it gets exciting: Purpose in Life (PiL) appears to be a remarkable ally in the battle against long-term stress. No matter our age, a high sense of PiL has the potential to counter the adverse effects of stress. It makes sense when you think about it; living a life filled with purpose, guided by our loving hearts, can positively change our cardiovascular system, our gut, and our emotional well-being.

Our hearts, both the emotional and physiological kind, hold the key to our overall well-being. Living a life infused with purpose not only feels incredible, but it also has no negative side

---

[33] Jillian McKoy, "Higher Sense of Purpose in Life May Be Linked to Mortality Risk," Boston University School of Public Health, accessed November 4, 2022, www.bu.edu/sph/news/articles/2022/sense-of-purpose-in-life-may-be-linked-to-mortality-risk.

effects. In fact, it has the potential to be our lifeline. PiL is more than just a feel-good sentiment; it's a transformative force. It enhances our quality of life and plays a pivotal role in extending it.

Unveiling the Key to Vibrant and Fulfilling Aging

As we conclude this section about PiL, we unveil a comprehensive study that serves as the perfect culmination of our exploration. Entitled "Purpose in Life in Adulthood and Older Adulthood: An Integrative Review," this study took over two years to meticulously select and analyze insights from thirty-two different research studies focused on PiL and healthy aging. The revelations from this integrative review are nothing short of amazing, shedding light on how a strong sense of purpose can be the key to vibrant and fulfilling aging. From improved self-care to cognitive resilience and protection against health issues, PiL is a tool in the quest for healthy and purposeful longevity.

This culmination of insights uncovered five key revelations that underscore PiL's pivotal role in promoting vibrant and fulfilling aging.

1. People with a strong sense of purpose take better care of themselves, learn new skills, socialize more, and enjoy meaningful activities. This positive outlook helps them see aging in a better light.
2. A strong sense of purpose (PiL) is associated with good mental traits like optimism and self-confidence. It's also linked to healthy habits, like exercising regularly and avoiding risky behaviors.
3. Having a sense of purpose in life (PiL) has been shown to protect against various health issues such as mortality, heart diseases, cognitive decline, functional limitations,

hospitalizations, and other negative outcomes. This effect stays consistent across different age groups.
4. Efforts to boost purpose in life (PiL) among seniors could help strengthen cognitive abilities and goal-driven actions. This shows promise in reducing cognitive decline and supporting overall healthy aging.
5. As people live longer, having a strong sense of purpose in life (PiL) becomes essential for both physical and mental well-being. It plays a vital role in guiding innovative approaches to promoting healthy aging.[34]

A Super Cool Retired Woman

Let me introduce you to a woman who truly has a strong PiL! Prepare to be inspired as we step into the world of Mickie Zada, founder of the Cool Retired Women's Club (CRWC). She is a remarkable individual who, at the age of seventy-plus, is living her dream and helping ignite the passions of thousands of women. I had the privilege of crossing paths with Mickie shortly after she launched this vibrant community in September 2019. At the time, its membership was much smaller, but under Mickie's warm, caring, and refreshingly honest leadership, it has grown to over forty-four thousand members and continues to flourish. Get ready to be moved and motivated by her incredible story as we discuss Mickie's extraordinary life, her vision for the CRWC, and the unwavering purpose that has propelled her to inspire and empower countless others.

Q: Mickie, one of your quotes is, "Your feelings and emotions are your strongest indicator if your life is moving in a purposeful

---

[34] Cristina Cristovão Ribeiro, MS Yassuda, and AL Neri, "Purpose in Life in Adulthood and Older Adulthood: An Integrative Review," *Cien Saude Colet* 25, no. 6 (June 2020): 2127–2142, doi:10.1590/1413-81232020256.20602018, Epub 2018 October 13. PMID: 32520260.

direction or not, so listen closely to how you feel." Does this quote still resonate with you?

Absolutely true! In my life, I didn't really live my life after age fifteen until I was fifty-three.

Q: What do you mean?

At fifty-three, I realized I wasn't living my life. Over all those years, I allowed another person to make my decisions. I married at the age of eighteen. After thirty-four years of marriage, I didn't even know what my favorite color was. I felt worn away like a stone in a creek, and over time, as the water washes over the stone, it gets worn away, yet the stone doesn't know it. If you do not listen to your feelings and emotions, you lose who you really are, and that is tragic.

Q: What happened when you were fifty-three?

Something happened, and I considered it to be an awakening. During that year, I began to rediscover myself. I left my husband, my marriage, and put myself into what I call a self-impaired repair shop for five years. I read books, joined a Unity Church, got therapy, and I got coaching. I realized I had to let go of my past to find myself. I knew if I didn't find me, I would lose myself again.

Q: What emotions and feelings had you been living with most of your adult life?

Fear and anxiety. I had no idea what a strong person I was. To the outside world, everything looked wonderful. Nice cars, beautiful home, successful career, and my ex-husband was a pillar of the community. At home it wasn't so beautiful.

Q: What are some of the insights and emotions that surprised you after your divorce?

I had to excavate myself. I had never been alone—I was afraid to be alone. But I discovered that I enjoyed being alone. In fact, I never thought I would ever marry again.

Q: When you talk about your life with your husband, Alan, you are always smiling. You appear to be so happy. Are you happy?

I never thought I would ever marry again, but I do believe in the law of attraction, and it was because of how I was living my life with purpose and in faith that he came into my life. And I couldn't be happier.

Q: About twenty-five years ago, you developed type two diabetes. Despite your mom having had it, you said you didn't understand why you had diabetes. Do you believe that living in chronic fear and anxiety contributed to developing diabetes?

Yes, I do believe it was secondary to my fear and anxiety. Louise Hay says, "You develop diabetes because you don't have enough sweetness in your life." Within three years of my diagnosis, I left my ex-husband. My mother was very thin, yet she had diabetes. Because of this, I believed I had to be thin to have diabetes. When I was diagnosed, I had gained fifty pounds and was overweight. Also, as soon as I was diagnosed with diabetes, I lost fifty pounds without trying. Crazy about the power of our thoughts and beliefs.

Q: What is your purpose in life?

My personal mission, and sometimes I call it a spiritual mission, is in faith and confidence to align with divine intent and serve as a beacon to other women. That is who I am, what I live for, and how I make decisions. Cool Retired Women came from living my purpose.

Q: What would you like to share to inspire others?

Discover who you are, and your purpose will serve as your North Star. The truth is, a lot of older women do not know they can change that.

Q: My life's purpose got shaken up after COVID-19, especially with all the restrictions and disconnection from others. In fact, this book was inspired by my own internal struggles, challenges, fears, and anxieties. How did this period affect you?

For almost twenty years, I have lived my life by divine intent. In September 2019, the idea of Cool Retired Women's Club came to me by divine intervention. Between the launch on Facebook that September and the worldwide lockdowns in March/April, CRWC had grown to a few thousand women. But since the lockdowns, it has grown beyond my wildest dreams.

Q: Why?

We had all lost friends and connections, but CRWC was a safe and open place. Now we have over forty-four thousand members from around the world, and it keeps growing.

Q: Do you feel you take better care of yourself and are more mindful of your health because of your commitment to your purpose, to those you serve?

My intention is to live to be one hundred and six. And to live to be one hundred and six, I need to take care of my body—to have a strong body and a good, strong brain. I need to keep my body healthy and my mind strong.

Thank you, Nancy.

Below, I have distilled the wisdom from Mickie Zada's inspiring journey into nine key takeaways. These takeaways serve as guiding lights, prompting us to reflect on our own lives, values, and aspirations. As you read each point, consider how they resonate with your experiences and how they might illuminate your path toward a more purposeful and fulfilling existence.

Listen to Your Emotions

Tune into your feelings and emotions because they are powerful indicators of whether you are moving in a purposeful direction. Mickie's journey underscores the significance of paying close attention to one's emotional compass. Otherwise, neglecting it can lead to a life lived without true purpose.

Take Control over Your Life Decisions

Do you have control over your life decisions, or have external influences played a significant role? Mickie's story is a poignant reminder that reclaiming control over one's life can be a transformative step toward living with purpose and authenticity.

Rediscover Yourself

When in your life have you felt the need for self-discovery or renewal? Mickie's story reveals that, while not easy, experiencing a period of rediscovering one's true self can reshape one's perspective on life.

Thoughts and Beliefs Are Powerful

Your thoughts and beliefs are powerful in shaping your experiences.

Define Your Personal Purpose

Reflecting on your personal purpose can guide your decisions and actions toward a more fulfilling life. Do you have a clear mission driving you, or are you still discovering it? Clarifying your purpose empowers you to align your choices with what truly matters to you.

Be an Inspiration

Embracing your authenticity and living in alignment with your values can inspire and motivate others to pursue their passions and ideals.

Acknowledge the Impact of Significant Life Events

Reflecting on significant life events, like the COVID-19 pandemic, offers insight into how they've influenced your sense of purpose, relationships, and personal growth. Consider the lessons learned from these experiences and how they can be integrated into your pursuit of a Purpose in Life (PiL).

Self-Care and Health

Prioritizing self-care and staying healthy are integral to achieving one's purpose and maximizing overall well-being. It's important to reflect on one's commitment to self-care and health in the pursuit of personal goals and purpose. Consideration of the steps taken to support oneself on this journey can lead to increased self-awareness and resilience.

Please see the Acknowledgments and Contact Information section at the end of the book for more details about Mickie Zada.

Integrating a Sense of Purpose into Your Best Life Ever!

Living life with purpose is an essential, I almost want to say non-negotiable, pillar to vibrant aging. Having a focus greater than ourselves is very powerful, for not just our hearts but for our cells.

As we discovered from the PiL research, this doesn't mean you have to aspire for some huge, lofty mission to save the world—it can be random acts of kindness to family, friends, and strangers, volunteering, or sharing your talents and gifts with others, just to name a few. Mickie started an online platform for women; my father gave what he could to nonprofits, family, and friends. One purpose is not better than another. But it must be from the heart and truly your purpose.

Living Life from a Heart Space and Embracing Vibrant Aging

Here are six key yet simple ways to integrate purpose into your life NOW!

Create a Daily Gratitude Practice

Each day, reflect on something you appreciate now or will appreciate in the near future. Some examples include the great time you had with friends, the fabulous book you're reading that's inspiring you, new opportunities, a new person you met, or an upcoming adventure. It's critical that you not take these things for granted, because reflecting with gratitude increases the chances that you'll continue to attract these good things.

Pay Attention to Your Emotions and Journal about Them

Aging is definitely not for sissies. Each of us has had full, amazing lives with many ups and downs, twists and turns. Embracing our emotions, both positive and negative, can be scary sometimes. But if you listen, they have something to tell you. Write them down. Journal. There will be great wisdom and insight if you simply allow yourself the grace to express yourself.

Rediscover Your Passion

What are you passionate about? Share it with the world! Is it being an amazing grandparent who can have wonderful adventures with your grandkids as they grow up? Are you passionate about teaching life lessons? A few years ago, I taught a vegan cooking class to inner-city kids (I'm not vegan now). It ended up being a type of survival class, because we sourced most of our ingredients from a local food pantry. I loved the teens and the opportunity to inspire them. Truthfully, when I'm in that space where I'm really using my passion, I often think, I hope they're gaining at least half as much from me as I'm gaining from them.

Connect with Others

Each of us loves being thought about. So spend time with family and friends. Join a local community group. Loneliness is a real problem, globally. So reach out and connect!

Practice Self-Care and Find Balance

Every day, do at least one thing that makes you smile and brings you some joy. This could be as simple as taking a warm bath, reading a book, listening to music, baking cookies for a friend, or going to a local exercise class.

Connect Your Passion with Service

As with passion, what truly makes your heart sing? Gardening and sharing your bounty with others, playing with grandchildren, loving your animals, volunteering (or being paid) within an organization or community? Discover this . . . embrace . . . share!

Remember that purpose isn't a fixed destination but a dynamic force that evolves with you. Embrace it, listen to your emotions, take control of your decisions, rediscover yourself, and let your thoughts and beliefs shape your path. Inspire others with your actions, learn from significant life events, and prioritize self-care and health while pursuing your purpose.

Living from a heart space and embracing vibrant aging involves gratitude, passion, connection, balance, and service. It's about appreciating the small moments, letting your heart sing, nurturing relationships, taking care of yourself, and sharing your unique gifts with the world. Your purpose doesn't have to be grand; it just needs to be from the heart—truly yours and truly fulfilling.

So, as you embark on this journey of vibrant aging with purpose as your compass, remember that it's not just about aging gracefully; it's about aging vibrantly, with a heart full of gratitude, a soul on fire with passion, and a life well-lived in service to others. Embrace your purpose, and let it be the driving force behind your best life ever.

PART THREE

Sagehood

CHAPTER 9

BECOMING A VIBRANT SAGE

*In the end, it's not the years in your life that count.
It's the life in your years.*
— Abraham Lincoln

Throughout the earlier chapters of this book, you've uncovered the vital pillars of vibrant aging—breath, movement, nutrition, sleep, and purpose. These pillars are the solid cornerstones for a life bursting with passion, energy, and vitality, regardless of the years that have passed.

But now, we embark on a deeper exploration of aging gracefully and vibrantly, a concept I fondly refer to as "Becoming a Vibrant Sage." Before we dive into this enlightening concept, allow me to share a story that may strike a chord with you.

Meet Janet, a woman in her early fifties who had always been full of life. She effortlessly tackled each day with enthusiasm, juggling work, family, and her love of the outdoors. Janet was known for her boundless energy, and her friends often marveled at her vitality.

But as the years passed, Janet felt a subtle shift. She noticed that she wasn't as energetic as she used to be. Climbing the stairs to her office felt like a chore, and she felt a little breathless afterward.

Her favorite hiking trails, once conquered with ease, now seemed daunting.

Janet had put on a few extra pounds, and her clothes no longer fit comfortably. Her doctor had gently mentioned the importance of healthy habits, but Janet had brushed it off, thinking she had plenty of time to make changes later.

One evening, as she watched a vibrant sunset with her loyal dog, Duke, by her side, Janet was captivated by the beauty of the moment. The sky painted in hues of orange and pink reminded her of the days when life felt like an endless adventure and she had been filled with boundless energy. But now, a subtle sense of longing had settled in her heart.

She missed the days when she had effortlessly danced through life, brimming with vigor and vitality. As the sun dipped below the horizon, she felt a gentle breeze whisper against her skin, almost as if it were urging her to pay attention to the quiet voice from within.

She realized she couldn't continue to ignore her body's whispers, the subtle hints that something needed to change. Yet Janet felt lost and overwhelmed, unsure of where to begin on this path of rejuvenation.

If only she had the book that you now hold in your hands.

Embrace the Sage Within

Welcome getting older not as a decline but as an ascent into a realm of wisdom, purpose, and boundless energy. This is the essence of a vibrant sage. Each one of us has the potential to become a sage, drawing from the rich tapestry of our life experiences, challenges, and lessons. It's about embracing the sage within you.

Consider the stories of those who have walked this path before you, individuals who, with the passing of time, discovered newfound vitality and a deep sense of purpose. Within this book, Michaël, Cathy, Dr. Karl, Dr. Allison Brager, Mickie, and my dad all stand for becoming a vibrant sage. They are the embodiment of vibrant sages, and their stories serve as inspiration for your journey.

The Five Pillars of Sagehood

The five pillars—breath, movement, nutrition, sleep, and purpose—lay the solid groundwork for vibrant aging. These pillars serve as the compass, guiding us toward a life brimming with vitality, passion, and energy. However, it's important to understand that they are not just about physical health; they're also powerful pathways to nurturing the mind and spirit.

A vibrant sage, someone who gracefully embraces the passage of time and the changes that go with it, recognizes that true vitality emerges from a harmonious balance of all these elements. It's about more than just preserving a youthful appearance or trying to turn back the clock. Instead, it's an acknowledgment of the beauty in the aging process, a celebration of the wisdom that comes with each passing year.

As we go through life, we inevitably face changes—both in our bodies and our circumstances. It's easy to become fixated on the desire to recapture the days of our youth, longing for the smooth skin and boundless energy that once defined us. But a vibrant sage knows that true vibrancy doesn't exist solely in the past; it thrives in the present and grows with each new day.

Heart-Centered Living as the Core

At the heart of becoming a vibrant sage is a heart-centered approach to life, and I don't just mean the physical organ that beats within your chest. I'm referring to the heart as the source of our ability to connect with others, to feel empathy, and to radiate positive energy. It's the epicenter of our emotional intelligence, the compass that guides us toward fulfilling our purpose.

The five pillars of vibrant aging promote physical health as well as nurture our emotional well-being. This connection between the physical and emotional realms is at the core of being vibrant and a sage.

Each pillar, in its unique way, contributes to heart health. Proper breathing calms the heart and reduces stress. Movement enhances circulation and keeps our hearts strong. Nutrition supports the body's functions, including the heart's vital work. Quality sleep rejuvenates both body and soul, allowing us to approach each day with a joyful heart. Purpose, perhaps the most significant pillar, is what ignites the fire within our hearts, inspiring us to live with passion and meaning.

It's this symbiotic relationship between the pillars and our emotional well-being that forms the foundation of becoming a vibrant sage. By nurturing your heart, both physically and emotionally, you unlock the true potential for a life that's not just vibrant, but wise, compassionate, and deeply fulfilling.

Sage Connections

As vibrant sages continue to live life to the fullest, something remarkable happens. They begin to emanate an aura of vibrancy, zest, and joy that's palpable to those around them. Their health and vitality become clear—not just in their appearance but also in their actions, words, and interactions.

People can't help but notice the sparkle in their eyes, the spring in their step, and the genuine smile that graces their faces. It's as if they've tapped into a wellspring of vitality that overflows into everything they do. Their laughter is infectious, and their energy seems boundless.

But what truly sets vibrant sages apart is their generosity of spirit. They've learned that true vibrancy goes hand in hand with giving back to others. Their lives are filled with a sense of purpose that extends beyond their personal goals and desires. They've discovered that the more they invest in their health and well-being, the more they have to offer their communities, loved ones, and the world.

Vibrant sages often become beacons of wisdom, support, and guidance for those around them. Their life experiences and lessons learned become the guiding light for others, illuminating the path toward a more fulfilling life. Their connections with others are rooted in empathy, understanding, and a deep desire to uplift those they meet.

People seek out vibrant sages for advice, not just on health but on life itself. They are trusted confidants, mentors, and pillars of strength during challenging times. And the beauty of it all is that vibrant sages are more than willing to share their knowledge and experiences because they understand that their journey isn't just about personal growth; it's about elevating the collective well-being of their communities.

Becoming a Sage Is a Lifelong Journey

The path to becoming a vibrant sage is not bound by age. It's a lifelong journey of self-discovery, growth, and continuous learning. Your sage-like qualities can flourish at any stage of life, provided you are still open to the possibilities and keep nurturing your heart and spirit.

The Sage's Legacy

As you aspire to become a vibrant sage, think about the legacy you want to leave behind. Your wisdom, values, and the positive impact you have on others will be your enduring legacy. Consider the ripple effect of your actions and how they can inspire and uplift future generations.

Embracing Vibrancy: The Journey to Becoming a Vibrant Sage

Embrace this concept of becoming a vibrant sage—an individual who ages with wisdom, passion, and purpose. Continue to nurture your heart, keep a balanced life, and share your wisdom with others. Your path to becoming a vibrant sage leads to a life of enduring fulfillment and boundless vitality.

Janet's Transformation: From Lost to Vibrant Sage

You met Janet at the beginning of this chapter. Now, I would like to share the vision I have for her—her transformation after reading this book, the same one you're reading now.

Janet had always heard the whispers from her body, urging her to act, but she didn't know where to begin. That is, until she found the book—your book—now well-worn and filled with notes, highlights, and dog-eared pages.

She devoured each chapter, absorbing the wisdom about the five pillars of vibrant aging—breath, movement, nutrition, sleep, and purpose. These pillars provided the structure for her transformation. Janet realized that these weren't just physical principles; they were pathways to nurturing her mind and spirit.

Breath became her anchor in times of stress, allowing her to stay present and connected with herself and others. Movement became her daily ritual, not just for physical health but as a way to explore the world with renewed vigor. Nutrition became a source of nourishment, not just for her body but also for her soul, as she savored each bite and shared meals with loved ones.

Sleep was her sanctuary, a time of rest and rejuvenation, where her body and mind healed. Purpose became her guiding star, inspiring her to live with intention, share her newfound vitality, and give back to her community.

With each passing day, Janet felt the transformation within. Her strength returned, and the extra pounds melted away as she embraced healthier habits within each pillar. Climbing the steps, once a struggle, became a joyful daily exercise. She was no longer tired and weak, but strong and vibrant.

But the most significant change was in Janet's attitude. She no longer longed for youth or tried to turn back the clock. She reveled in the journey of aging gracefully, cherishing every moment, and letting go of unrealistic expectations. She understood that becoming a vibrant sage was about embracing life at every stage, not trying to recapture the past.

People couldn't help but notice the profound change in Janet. Her aura radiated vibrancy, and her zest for life was contagious. Friends and family marveled at her newfound energy and became inspired to make positive changes in their lives too.

Janet had become a wellspring of wisdom, support, and guidance for those around her. Her connections with others deepened, rooted in empathy, understanding, and a genuine desire to uplift those she met. She had become a vibrant sage, not just in body but in spirit.

One evening, as she watched another vibrant sunset with her faithful dog by her side, Janet felt a profound sense of gratitude.

She knew her journey was far from over, but she also knew she was on the right path—a path of vibrancy, purpose, and connection.

And as the sun dipped below the horizon, Janet couldn't help but smile, take a deep breath, and say, "Feels so good to be alive."

What will be your unique journey to becoming a vibrant sage?

CHAPTER 10

PASSION AND INTIMACY: THE POWER OF CONNECTION AND SEXUALITY

If sexuality is one dimension of our ability to live passionately ... then in cutting off our sexual feelings we diminish our overall power to feel, know, and value deeply.

— JUDITH PLASKOW

Have you ever paused to consider the intricate web of connections that shape your life?

Connections with ourselves, our loved ones, our world, and even those intimate connections that stir our deepest passions. In this chapter, we're embracing a realm that's both profoundly personal and universally relatable—connection and sexuality.

Life is like a beautifully woven tapestry, with each thread representing a different aspect of our existence. The threads of breath, movement, nutrition, sleep, and purpose, which we've explored in earlier chapters, are interwoven into this intricate design. They influence how we breathe, move, eat, rest, and find purpose in our lives.

Now, let's zoom in on the thread of connection. Connection isn't just another thread; it's the glue that binds the others together. It's what transforms the act of breathing into mindful awareness, movement into a dance of life, nutrition into nourishment for body and soul, sleep into rejuvenation, and purpose into a journey shared with others.

Without connection, even the healthiest lifestyle can leave us feeling adrift, isolated, and incomplete, regardless of our age. It's a universal truth that spans generations.

As we navigate the chapters of our lives, one of the most profound expressions of connection is found in the realm of sexuality. In our early years, a fiery biological drive within us propels us toward reproduction. But as we age, especially for post-menopausal women, the reasons for our sexual connections evolve. They become about more than procreation; they become about intimacy, pleasure, and the fulfillment of our deepest desires.

Did you know that the practices and principles we've explored in the five pillars have a profound impact on not just our physical health but also our sexual vitality? A healthier body and heart can make the experience of sexual connection richer and more fulfilling.

Let's get a better understanding of the profound interplay between connection and sexuality and how they both play crucial roles in our journey toward vibrant aging.

Sexuality and Vibrancy: An Interview with a Sex Therapist

When I started writing this book, my first thought was to explore the intriguing notion of "happy horny cells" leading to a "happy horny life." The concept of "horny cells" essentially refers to cells that are vibrant, youthful, and full of life, mirroring the state

PASSION AND INTIMACY: THE POWER OF CONNECTION AND SEXUALITY

of our overall health. It seemed like common sense to me that a healthier individual would naturally experience a better sex life. However, recognizing that I'm not a sex therapist, I realized that along with providing you with the motivation to embrace a healthy lifestyle that integrates the principles of the five pillars, I needed to offer the expertise of a distinguished professional in the field who could shed light on this fascinating connection between vitality and sexuality. So I sought out Stephanie P. Bathurst, PhD, LCMFT, CPLC, CIMHP, CKCT. Dr. Bathurst is a renowned therapist, healer, sexologist, and coach, boasting an impressive array of credentials. She holds certifications as a TCA board-certified clinical sexologist, AAMFT licensed marriage and family therapist, certified integrative mental health professional, CLCI certified professional life coach, and certified kink-conscious therapist.

In this interview, Dr. Stephanie shares her profound insights into the intricate relationship between sexuality and vibrant aging. Her expertise offers a fresh perspective on how embracing the five pillars of vibrant aging can enhance not only your overall health but also your sexual well-being. So let's dive into this enlightening conversation, where you'll discover how nurturing your vitality can lead to a more fulfilling and passionate life, both inside and outside the bedroom.

Q: What did you think about the quote, "If sexuality is one dimension of our ability to live passionately in the world then in cutting off our sexual feelings, we diminish our overall power to feel, know, and value deeply," from Judith Plaskow?

It resonated with me. We're all sexual creatures. It is evolutionary and how we are built. Rejecting sexuality, sensuality, romance, or just our inherent desire to belong to a social system that's bigger than us ends up creating internal strife within us because we're trying to be something or someone that we just aren't biologically built for.

Q: Why do you think sexuality can be a challenge as we age?

There's this misconception that overt and open sexual expression is symbolic of immaturity or underdevelopment in secure attachments within a relationship. It's accepted when you are youthful, but when you're older, not so much. Often it is frowned upon. I intend to shatter that misconception and help people embrace that side of themselves. Sexual intimacy is a profound part of healthy relationships and a critical part of life, or like a healthy individuated being.

Q: You are so right. Why is sexuality as you age not as accepted by some people?

Sex is a superficial expression of behavior that is more grounded in conservatism, religion, or some prism of American history. Here we are in the twenty-first century, and some of that is overlapping into our culture today. We are still working against that.

Q: Could you share more about the importance of sex for our health and well-being?

Sex teaches us a lot about ourselves and the world around us. It gives us a consistent opportunity to synchronize our mind and body. It activates the production of hormones to improve health and immunity. It literally heals pain in the body. It helps us communicate our wants and boundaries with other people, which are critical communication skills. It helps us assess social situations for safety and appropriateness. It helps us to embrace our individuality, our own body form and desires, and really just experience

PASSION AND INTIMACY: THE POWER OF CONNECTION AND SEXUALITY

great pleasure and attachment with another person. These are all components of quality of life that we would be without, without sex.

Q: The first title of this book was *Happy Horny Cells, Happy Horny Life*. The underlying theme was to empower adults, especially after fifty, to vibrance and to lead a healthy lifestyle. Yet during market research, I discovered most men were intrigued, almost giddy sometimes, while over half the women surveyed were not interested in the topic of sex at all, or maybe they denied interest. Why do you think that was?

First, realize not all women struggle with their sexuality or being sensual. But there are psychological and physiological factors that have a profound impact on many women. There is first the mindset about the way your body looks—you can be embarrassed. Menopause also creates changes. Your hormones change, which has a profound impact on your ability to get aroused. Foreplay and lubrication are great tools to mitigate this challenge.

Q: Why do we struggle so much with the changes in our sexual being as we age?

Knowledge is so important. So much information is given in normative culture and social media that is very much backed by the pharmaceutical companies, which are a white male-dominated culture. That is NOT helping us as a group, as a demographic. We are not getting the information that we need about the developmental stages in our life, what our bodies go through, and how we can normalize that and feel okay about those experiences rather than shame them. It doesn't help us come together and feel socially connected as we age. There is so much shame wrapped up with sex and sensuality, especially as we get past, I would say, thirty and above.

Q: Our thirties seem so young; I would have thought maybe forty-five to fifty.

Once we start having children, our roles and dynamics in the family start to shift. And the expectation of our outside systems is that we prioritize being a parent and a partner over being a sexual being. It doesn't have to be that black and white, that binary. Providing education about our bodies and sharing our experiences is important so that we can shatter unhelpful and damning ideologies.

Q: So when you're younger, you tend to be more sexual and more vibrant, and then you have your family, and things begin to shift. It seems like so many stages in our lives are pre-planned. You know, you go to school, you go to college, you get a job, you get married. I mean, it might sound traditional, but it's true. And then you get older, forties and fifties, and you ponder, who am I, where did I go, where did that twenty-year-old go? Ultimately, I want my readers to rediscover their passion and excitement for life again. To feel it NOW!

No matter the age!

That is why sexuality is so important, because if you take that away, it feels like you're really missing out on something. *Sexuality is much more than sex;* the actions of sex, which is just one part—the physical act. But that is not what sex is as a whole. The act of sex—physical touch and affection—connects us at a deep psychological and emotional level. Sexuality, sensuality, intimacy, and connectedness are complex and deeply biological, at

PASSION AND INTIMACY: THE POWER OF CONNECTION AND SEXUALITY

a cellular level, things that are inherent and intrinsic within us as creatures. That doesn't just go away. Those are needs that are within us. They're ingrained. So, when we remove them or when we deprioritize them for long, extended periods of time, we feel that starvation. When we have young children, we can all kind of feel the familiarity of being over touched. Our children are on top of us all the time. But when we think about the exact opposite of being under touched or not touched for long periods of time, there is a feeling of scarcity and a need for physical affection, and it hits you deep, to the core, like a pit in your stomach. Over time, when those needs don't get met, it affects you, and it's much more than saying, "That's kind of a bummer, but I'm going to keep going on my way," as if it's just a superficial behavior. It is so much more complex than just an action. We get into that as we talk more about sacred sexuality in the context of tantric sex and more like Eastern philosophies of sexuality—connectedness to spirituality. It's multidimensional.

Q: My first pillar is about breath. When I was citing sources about breath and sexuality, they revealed that when you breathe properly, it helps to reduce blood pressure—the cardiovascular system works better—so then a man is better able to have an erection. Additionally, sources revealed that using the breath can strengthen your connection with the other person. So that's more, I guess, in the tantric area. How do you think breathing helps with sex or with your cells?

There are so many different aspects for how breath is not just valuable but actually critically important for sex. First, the cardiovascular system. For men, erectile functioning and sustainability, and for women, the physiological arousal. Both of those processes are dependent on the flood of blood and your need to breathe.

Regulate deep breaths so your blood vessels do not become constricted and constrained, which is super important. Consistency of breathing prevents exhaustion and muscle cramping. By encouraging that during sex and beforehand, you are gaining continuous oxygenation throughout the experience into your bodily systems for sexual play so that you can enjoy the experience and not interrupt it.

Q: Is that why you sometimes get a cramp during sex, like in your leg or something?

Oftentimes, it is. Once you're getting to the peak of orgasm, all your muscles are contracting, and that includes your breath muscles. Your body stops carrying oxygen to the other vital organs of your body, and everything needs oxygen consistently all the time. Another aspect of breath being super valuable is that it's used actually as a muscle to enhance the fluidity of movements.

Pilates is my primary source of fitness and exercise. I'm very familiar with this concept of breath being used as a muscle. When you practice exhaling, activate your core muscles, your abs, and your pelvic floor, it helps increase not just orgasm strength, but it also prevents minor injuries during sexual play, such as your lower back going out. Because all of your core muscles are now being activated together and working in synchrony with one another. And that's all happening because you are activating deep core breathing in those moments. So, you prevent injury, and you increase your orgasm strength and responsiveness, which is amazing.

Q: Pilates is a fabulous form of exercise/movement at any age. Thanks for sharing. The second pillar is movement. If you don't have movement, I don't think you can have sex. When I did

PASSION AND INTIMACY: THE POWER OF CONNECTION AND SEXUALITY

my research and I talked about science, I found that movement also has a profound impact on the cardiovascular system. And I talk a little bit about flexibility, strength, endurance. What are important factors that people need to know about the relationship between perfecting your sexual health or your sex life and movement?

Sex is a form of exercise. It requires energy, exertion, and there's a recovery period that your body needs afterward in order to recuperate and manage some of the muscle development. There is a recuperation afterward. Optimizing your fitness, your movement, is only going to improve your sexual experience for a myriad of reasons. When you increase your cardio on a regular basis, you're increasing your stamina and endurance in the sexual play realm. If you are moving your body on a regular basis, and you're stretching, you develop confidence, and you trust your body in certain positions. Then you're able to bring that kind of confidence into the bedroom. Conversely, if you aren't practicing that outside, the confidence is low, the anxiety is probably high. Anxiety is one of the prominent sources of erectile dysfunction and miscommunication or relationship conflict during sex. We need to remove any obstacles that promote anxiety. Trusting and being connected to your own body is a direct way to eliminate or reduce some of those anxieties that we as individuals bring into those sexual intimacy experiences.

Q: I enjoy providing personal training to couples. It's such a great way to help others be more playful while improving their health and supporting each other. At least ninety percent of the time, they leave smiling and happy. Such a powerful way to connect. I wish more couples worked out together.

Playfulness is key! It is being able to be in a fun and vulnerable space rather than having your protective mechanisms or your defense mechanisms up and trying to look good all the time. When you can feel like your true, genuine self, and your partner feels that authenticity, it can be powerful. Playfulness is absolutely key in the fitness realm, in the sexual realm, in wherever you are, and in everything.

Q: Why is morning sex important?

Morning sex is actually really important. I've been talking about that particular piece of the puzzle for so long. Many people have it in their mind that sex is normal after work, at the very end of the day, when our energy and hormone levels are so depleted. Sleep is what regenerates all of the hormone levels. Testosterone is highest when you wake up in the morning. That is the moment to be engaging with one another if you're able to. Waking up with an erection is a sign of healthy levels of testosterone. For women, if they're able to check in with their bodies, which we're encouraging that level of mind-body connection and awareness, we'll notice that they're open as well. More so than in the evening after they've been taxed all day. And that's because your hormone levels have been replenished.

Q: The third pillar is nutrition. I shared a list of different foods that are good for sexual health. I discovered that, ultimately, it's good for your cardiovascular system. But how are nutrition and sex connected? Does what you eat make a difference in your sexual experience?

Absolutely. Let's start with the microbiome. Your microbiome is going to impact the production or the inability to produce everything else in your body. Which means you need to be very mindful of the inflammatory foods that you're putting into your body. By high-inflammatory foods, I mean you need to be mindful of gluten and dairy, as well as nightshades. You need to know what, if any, foods you may be allergic to. Many people have problems with these, as evidenced by gas and GI challenges. Everyone should dramatically reduce or eliminate highly processed foods. We don't always recognize the signs that our bodies are communicating to us, but if we're having inflammatory responses in our system, it's absolutely going to affect our ability to positively respond to physical stimuli. Do you know why? Because sex is not a priority. If your body is perceiving something as an active risk or threat, sex is secondary to survival. If our system is saying, wait, we are in active threat right now, everything else has to shut down, which means the sympathetic nervous system is turned on, that's the fight, flight, or freeze. So high anxiety or high histamine responses, whatever is turning your nervous system on into that level of like activation. It means the parasympathetic nervous system, which is the rest, digest, and sex nervous system, is essentially turned off or more difficult to activate. So essentially, everything that you eat can affect your ability to experience or tap into sexual responses if it's encouraging sympathetic nervous system responses.

Q: Do you recommend any specific supplements or nutrients?

I'm not going to give the dosing because I think it's unique for everybody. Vitamin D3 is very important—it's also most bioavailable when consumed with something because it is fat soluble. Also, trace minerals such as zinc, manganese, and magnesium are very important. Without these trace minerals, our bodies are not able to produce the building blocks, like amino acids, that we need for the production of very important hormones.

Q: How about the connection between sleep and sex? Many sources show that at least thirty-five percent of Americans don't sleep very well.

I think that number is very low. It has to be higher than thirty-five percent. Clients come to me with multiple presenting issues, all deserving attention. But if we were to attend to, say, all seven presenting issues, we could spend seven years in therapy, right? If we just attend to the first or the core presenting issue and resolve that, sometimes these secondary problems resolve on their own. Oftentimes, the core presenting issue is chronic sleep deprivation. Our bodies need sleep, and they need a good amount of sleep in order to replenish and recuperate. Our bodies are like a factory. If it's running twenty-four-seven and it doesn't have time to get the parts oiled or old parts repaired, it's going to just shatter and burn out, and the production line's not going to work anymore. We need time to decompress and to turn off so that our cells can repair and regenerate so that our hormone levels can replenish to their best levels or even functional levels. Without that, we're burning out chronically, and that changes everything.

Q: Is it true that having an orgasm before bed can help with sleep?

Definitely! The post-orgasm stage does promote sleep because you're exhausted after having contracted all of your muscles. It's kind of like progressive muscle relaxation, but in a much more glorious kind of way. Think about it, you are contracting everything so intensely, and then you've just released all of this pent-up energy within your body—it feels really relaxing and mentally clarifying for many people. If you're looking for a holistic route to better sleep, go for sex with your partner or with yourself.

PASSION AND INTIMACY: THE POWER OF CONNECTION AND SEXUALITY

Q: The last pillar is purpose. Have you ever thought about, or have you seen in your practice, any correlation between sex or healthy sex or feeling good about yourself sexually and how you view yourself in the world around you?

Yes, but in a reverse way. When you have a life filled with purpose that's aligned with personal integrity and authenticity, you feel better about yourself. That confidence can make its way into the bedroom. Conversely, when you feel disconnected from yourself, you absolutely aren't able to feel connected to somebody else during sex. Discovering and practicing your purpose in life encourages authenticity, integrity, and general connection to your own personality. You bring that kind of alignment and synchronicity into your sexual experiences. I think the pillar of living with purpose is fantastic. It comes full circle to the expansiveness of sex. It's beyond just a particular behavior or action. It can be a part of your identity and a part of your meaning in life, your existence in this world. For many of us, once we begin to understand who we are, what we need, and what we want out of life experiences, as long as we are acting intentionally, conscientiously, effortfully rather than mindlessly, sex is going to be great.

Q: What do you mean by "sex is going to be great"? Does that mean no awkward moments?

Real sex is not like what you see in the movies, with no awkward moments. That is not real sex. The key is that you and your partner both step into a space authentically, with pure intention, presence, and engagement. When that happens, there is not much that can go wrong.

Q: You are obviously very passionate about what you're doing. What got you into what you're doing now?

Since elementary school, I wanted to be a therapist. I love learning and am deeply intrigued by the complexity of people. My story is of unfailing passion and loyalty and commitment to this career. When working with couples, I believe you do the couple a disservice by not bringing sex, sexual intimacy, and physical affection into the mix, which is why I began getting trained in clinical sexology and eventually got my PhD. I love what I do, and what I do is help people heal hurt and embrace love.

Q: How does a healthy body and mind improve sex and intimacy?

Fun, functional movement. If you have good physical health, or at least you're not getting consistently injured, you are better able to manage positioning. This is very important. When movement is limited, sex can get boring. That is one of the reasons couples come to my room. They are so bored with the same type of sex, on the same day, at the same time, in the same room.

Q: How does an unhealthy body impact sex?

This can really create major challenges. You can become very upset and frustrated because you are limited to maybe only one to two positions because everything else causes discomfort or pain. Additionally, body image has an impact because when you do not feel good about your body, you become nervous about what your partner will think about your body.

Q: What should a person do in this situation?

First, talk about it. You MUST get all those thoughts and internal chatter out of your head and talk about it. When there are physical challenges, I may refer my client to a physical or occupational therapist to improve overall health, strength, and mobility.

PASSION AND INTIMACY: THE POWER OF CONNECTION AND SEXUALITY

Sometimes you need to learn ways to adapt and be creative. As you feel healthier, you can become more adventurous and bring spice into the mix.

Q: How about when a partner no longer finds the other attractive?

So many clients have expressed their love for their partner yet feel guilty that they no longer find them attractive. This can be a very difficult conversation. We have to find a way to talk about that and to manage that together. A healthy body does have a positive impact on sex and intimacy. It's not being skinny, it's feeling like your body is healthy; it's feeling like perhaps you have some tone and you feel strong and confident. There is a trust and confidence when you feel good about your body, which allows you to get into a flow state with yourself and your partner, which is so wonderful.

Q: What is the impact of anxiety on sex?

People with high anxiety may never have ever experienced a flow state in sex. When you trust your body and allow it to do its thing, rather than pre-calculating every single movement ahead of time, sex is much more pleasurable. Conversely, anxiety or overthinking can cause a sensation of being removed from the experience, almost as if you are floating above it rather than being in it. The actual orgasm may be pleasurable, but the process of getting up to it is probably not going to be. And that's a shame, because a healthy body can get you to the trust and the confidence that will allow you to really enjoy every ounce of that process.

Q: Is it true that many women don't orgasm?

Yes. However, the statistics on what a lot of women experience are highly variable, depending on what study you look at. With the increase of SSRIs and certain medications that are making it much more difficult for orgasms and even just physiological arousal to occur, in women in particular, it's complicating things. This can be a real barrier in relationships.

Q: Wow, what do you suggest a person do when they are challenged with physiological arousal?

There are holistic protocols that can manage and mitigate some of the medication-induced sexual dysfunction.

Q: You have brought up anxiety a few times. Are you finding that that's becoming a really pervasive problem?

One-hundred percent! Let me provide you with some examples of how anxiety is built in and interwoven into relationship issues pretty profoundly. For example, feeling anxious that your partner is cheating or anxiety and response to earlier infidelity can have an extreme impact on sex. Even from past experience, this can be an unhealed recovery. Or anxiety about body form or perceived judgment from other people. This is particular, but not exclusive, to women. For men, it's more about performance anxiety—being able to keep and sustain an erection during the entirety of sexual performance. What many people don't realize is that there is anxiety associated with pornography usage and masturbation and how that conditioning response really disrupts sexual experience within their partnership, which is its own separate ballgame we could spend hours talking about. Anxiety is a huge part as to where that conditioning response starts. A person may feel anxious about engaging or starting with their partner and feeling rejected. Consequently, it's easier to watch porn, masturbate, take

PASSION AND INTIMACY: THE POWER OF CONNECTION AND SEXUALITY

care of yourself, and get it over with because it's predictable, and you are fully in control of the situation. There are no social experiences that can promote anxiety or discomfort. Anxiety is built into almost all of these unhealthy or problematic sexual issues in different ways.

Q: Is there anything you'd like to share that I haven't asked about or that you want to reiterate as important, or things that are really valuable that should go into this book?

One of the biggest misnomers is that as we age, sex has to be boring and predictable. Aging together as a couple means, oftentimes, lessening a lot of major responsibilities, like managing children or stepping into retirement. These are pretty profound developmental life stages that can afford certain freedoms to the relational system, which you might not have had for decades.

These are amazing opportunities and times to try out new sexual styles, and explore new types of touch, and play and tune into your body, and reconnect sensually. This new freedom offers a great opportunity to explore something new, but unfortunately, many couples or individuals just don't take that chance, because previous to those transitions have been prolonged periods without physical affection. Often you are going from one extreme to the next. Yet for those who do see the opportunity and take it, I often see these developmental stages being synonymous with an openness to discuss and explore new relationship structures outside of traditional monogamy or getting more adventurous with your sexual style. It's so fun, creative, and freeing. And I want people to feel that kind of freedom because they've earned it. They have worked really hard and gotten to a place in life where they can choose whatever kind of relationship and whatever kind of sex best suits them. This can be a fun and playful period in their life. It doesn't have to be boring and predictable. There are many reasons, and that is just one.

> *Older often means wiser. Wiser does not have to mean more reserved. Have fun! Love your life! Get a little messy! Don't just survive, but actually live it.*
> — STEPHANIE BATHURST, PHD

The interview with Dr. Stephanie Bathurst offers valuable insights into the relationship between sexuality, health, and aging. Here are the key takeaways from the interview:

Sexuality Is Inherent

Sexuality is a fundamental aspect of being human, deeply ingrained in our biology. Rejecting or ignoring this aspect of ourselves can lead to internal conflicts and dissatisfaction.

Challenges in Aging

As people age, there can be misconceptions and societal pressures that diminish the acceptance and expression of sexuality. She aims to challenge these misconceptions and help individuals embrace their sexual selves at any age.

Societal Stigmas

Societal norms, conservatism, and historical influences can contribute to the lack of acceptance of sexuality in older age. These factors need to be addressed to promote a healthier view of sexuality in aging individuals.

Sex and Health

Sex has a profound impact on our overall health. It can help synchronize the mind and body, improve hormone production, and

PASSION AND INTIMACY: THE POWER OF CONNECTION AND SEXUALITY

even alleviate physical pain. Additionally, it enhances communication skills, boundaries, and social assessment.

Connection and Sex

Sex is a powerful form of connection, intimacy, and affection. It goes beyond the physical act and plays a role in strengthening emotional bonds between partners.

Breath and Sex

Proper breathing is crucial for sexual health. It supports cardiovascular functioning, enhances stamina, and reduces the risk of injuries. Deep, regulated breathing is essential for the best sexual experiences.

Movement and Sex

Regular physical activity and flexibility are essential for supporting an active and fulfilling sex life. Confidence and trust in one's body can lead to more adventurous and enjoyable experiences.

Morning Sex

Morning sex can be particularly beneficial because testosterone levels are highest in the morning. It's an opportunity for both partners to experience heightened arousal and connection.

Nutrition and Sex

Nutrition plays a significant role in sexual health. A balanced diet that minimizes inflammatory foods can positively affect arousal and responsiveness.

Sleep and Sex

Quality sleep is crucial for overall health and sexual well-being. Chronic sleep deprivation can lead to various issues, including reduced sexual desire and performance.

Orgasms and Sleep

Having an orgasm before sleep can promote relaxation and help with falling asleep. It allows individuals to release tension and experience a sense of mental clarity.

Sex and Purpose

A sense of purpose in life can enhance confidence and authenticity. It positively influences sexual experiences by promoting alignment and synchronicity in relationships.

Overcoming Challenges

Anxiety is a common challenge that affects sexual experiences. Open communication, seeking help when needed, and addressing anxiety-related issues can lead to a more fulfilling sex life.

Embracing Change

As people age and transition through different life stages, it's essential to embrace change and view it as an opportunity for growth and exploration. Sexuality doesn't have to diminish with age; it can evolve and become more creative.

Fun and Freedom

Aging offers newfound freedom to explore and experiment with one's sexuality and relationships. It's an opportunity to break free from traditional norms and discover what works best for each individual.

PASSION AND INTIMACY: THE POWER OF CONNECTION AND SEXUALITY

What is your key takeaway(s) from the interview with Dr. Bathurst?
Good sex is always filled with energy and vibrancy!

Please see the Acknowledgments and Contact Information section at the end of the book for more details about Dr. Stephanie P. Bathurst.

Sex, Connection, and the Five Pillars

"Breath and Sex," "Movement and Sex," "Food and Sex," "Sleep and Sex," and "Purpose and Sex"—these are the five pillars that not only support our overall well-being but also have a profound influence on our sexuality. As Dr. Bathurst reminds us, a healthy and vibrant sex life is within reach for all ages. It's about embracing change and exploring new possibilities.

Pillar 1: Breath and Sex

Your breath is not only a calming force for your nervous system but also a companion in your most intimate moments. It can heighten your experience and prevent disruptive cramping, ensuring that pleasure is uninterrupted.

Pillar 2: Movement and Sex

Strength, flexibility, and endurance provide the foundation for sexual exploration. You're never too old to get stronger, and professionals are available to help you achieve your fitness goals and overcome any obstacles affecting your sex life.

Pillar 3: Food and Sex

The right foods fuel a healthy, strong body, while the wrong ones can leave you feeling uncomfortable and bloated. Some foods even add an element of fun to foreplay, creating a delightful connection between nourishment and intimacy.

Pillar 4: Sleep and Sex

Quality sleep is essential for hormonal balance. Remember, testosterone is at its peak in the morning. Now that you have the flexibility to connect with your partner whenever the mood strikes, you can fully enjoy the benefits of your sleep.

Pillar 5: Purpose and Sex

A life filled with purpose brings positivity, self-assurance, and a deeper connection to the world. This mindset naturally extends to your intimate moments, creating a more profound experience. And, of course, there's the heart—the foundation that supports these five pillars. While sex isn't always about lovemaking, it is about connection. It's this connection that forms the bedrock upon which the five pillars stand.

Bringing the Five Pillars Plus Connection to Life
Rekindling the Flame

Meet Sarah and David, a couple in their early fifties who have been married for over twenty-five years. Like many long-term couples, their relationship had seen its fair share of ups and downs. They had built a life together, raised children, and navigated the challenges that life threw their way. However, somewhere along the way, they had lost the spark that once ignited their love.

Years of career demands, parenting responsibilities, and the busyness of everyday life had taken a toll on their connection. They became more like roommates than passionate partners. The emotional intimacy they once shared seemed to have faded away, and their physical connection had become routine and infrequent.

One day, as they were going through old photo albums and reminiscing about their early years together, Sarah and David came across a picture of their younger selves, beaming with joy on their honeymoon. That photo stirred something inside them, a longing to recapture the passion and connection they once had.

Inspired by the memory of their early days, they decided to take steps to rekindle their flame. They started by prioritizing quality time together, setting aside moments for deep conversations where they truly listened to each other's thoughts and dreams. They rediscovered the power of touch, holding hands, cuddling, and sharing affectionate gestures that had been absent for so long.

They also explored new experiences together, reigniting their sense of adventure. Whether it was taking up dance lessons, planning romantic getaways, or simply stargazing on their backyard deck, they found that these shared moments brought them closer than ever.

As they nurtured their emotional intimacy, their physical connection naturally followed suit. They learned that intimacy wasn't just about physical attraction but about feeling emotionally close and secure with one another. With open communication and a renewed commitment to their relationship, they reignited the passion that had been dormant for years.

Sarah and David's story serves as a reminder that with effort, communication, and a shared commitment to connection, couples can revitalize their love, no matter how long they've been together. Their efforts to rediscover intimacy showed them that it's never too late to nurture the bond that brought them together in the first place.

As you reflect on the five pillars to becoming a vibrant sage and their impact on your sexuality, consider how you can integrate them into your life. What changes can you make to achieve a healthier, more vibrant, and more fulfilling sex life? The journey begins with understanding the interconnectedness of these pillars and their role in supporting your sexual well-being.

Embrace change, explore new horizons, and remember that a vibrant sex life is a lifelong adventure. By nurturing your breath, movement, nutrition, sleep, purpose, and heart, you're taking vital steps toward a healthier, more passionate, and more gratifying life—in and out of the bedroom.

May your life be filled with energy, vibrancy, and the pleasures of a satisfying sex life.

CHAPTER 11

YOUR FUTURE IS NOW

The past is behind, learn from it.
The future is ahead, prepare for it.
The present is here, live it.
— Thomas S. Monson

My life was once driven by a relentless pursuit of fitness and a passion for running. It seemed like the path to health and vitality, but little did I know that it would lead to my downfall. It was a fateful day when I tore my labrum, and I found myself defeated, confused, and broken. But in that moment, when I faced adversity, I discovered the spark that would change my life forever.

If it weren't for my unwavering determination, my willingness to push through pain, cramping, and fatigue, I might never have embarked on the transformative journey to becoming a vibrant sage. This book might never have come into existence because, without that pivotal moment, I could have continued down a path of self-destruction, all in the name of "health."

I had a critical choice to make: keep moving forward while embracing significant changes, or give up on exercise altogether. Quitting was never in my nature. Instead, I did what I've always done when faced with the unknown—I started researching. I tried to understand what had happened to my body and explore ways to regain genuine health and vitality.

Over the next two to three years, I made remarkable progress, especially by transforming my exercise routine to focus more on strength training and nonimpact cardio like cycling. But my real breakthrough came when I uncovered the power of our uniqueness, driven by our genetic makeup encoded in our DNA. It was an aha moment when I realized the importance of listening to our bodies and embracing our inherent uniqueness, knowing that it evolves throughout our lives, influenced by factors like age, health, environment, relationships, and family dynamics.

My DNA revealed an inclination toward endurance activities, particularly long-distance running. Instead of pursuing this directly, I channeled my innate energy into coaching cycling and aqua aerobic classes. People often marvel at my boundless vitality, humorously commenting that "someone must have robbed the cradle" when they discover I have a teenage grandson. A decade ago, I couldn't have imagined having this level of energy and vibrancy. But in the past ten years, especially since 2017, I've committed to listening more attentively to my body, embracing my genetic advantages, and addressing potential disadvantages through dietary enhancements like antioxidants, vitamin D, and omega-3.

Today, in June 2024, I'm happily married to a man who shares my passion and enthusiasm for life, health, and living with an open heart. Our life together has been filled with mutual support as we've pursued our respective paths of growth and well-being.

This transformative journey, while definitely fulfilling, has had its share of challenges, struggles, and hurdles. Life, especially in the wake of the world-changing events of 2020, has thrown us curveballs that we've had to navigate. I've faced my own battles, wrestling with imposter syndrome while penning this book about my experiences and grappling with periods of depression that clouded my path.

My professional life has evolved from dedicated speech pathologist to personal trainer, health coach, and now, a Vibrant Aging Coach. These shifts, while ultimately rewarding, have been punctuated by moments of uncertainty and self-doubt.

But here's the universal truth: struggles and challenges are inherent in the human experience. Stress and fear often loom large, yet I firmly believe that we hold the power to triumph over these obstacles. By wholeheartedly embracing the five pillars of health, along with the profound strength of connection, we can create habits that uplift us in body, mind, soul, and life itself.

These habits are not just routines; they are practices deeply ingrained in our being, difficult to relinquish. Each new day offers a fresh opportunity to engage in these healthy habits that not only inspire us but also empower us. Once they become the sturdy foundation upon which we build our lives, they provide the vibrancy we need to live life on our own terms.

As we navigate the hurdles and embrace the transformative journey ahead, let these habits be the guiding lights that lead us to a more vibrant, purposeful existence.

And now, as we come full circle, I stand before you as a Vibrant Sage. Through trials, tribulations, and triumphs, I've come to understand that life is a remarkable, challenging, and ceaseless voyage of self-discovery.

So, I ask you:

Ten years ago, *what were your dreams, passions, and aspirations? Have you followed your heart and pursued them? Where has the last decade taken you? What transformations have you experienced in your body, your dreams, and your connection with yourself and your life?*

Reflecting on these questions can be the first step in your transformation to a vibrant and fulfilling life.

As you reach the conclusion of this book, I invite you to go on a profound journey—a journey within yourself. Take a moment to reflect on your path, your dreams, and the changes you wish to make. Picture your life in one year, five years, and even a decade from now. Envision your vibrant, energetic self living with purpose. While we can be realistic about the passing of time, remember that there may be new antiaging strategies in the future that you'll be able to embrace.

Recall the five pillars we've explored throughout this book: breath, movement, nutrition, sleep, and purpose. These pillars are your keys to a healthier, more fulfilling life. It doesn't matter where you start; what matters is that you begin. Choose the pillar or pillars that resonate most with you, those that will have the greatest impact not only on your life right now but also on your future.

Consider the stories of those who have embraced these pillars: Sam, who reclaimed his breath; Michaël, who overcame eczema through the power of breath; Cathy, who used mindful exercise to conquer her pain; Minerva, who prepared for retirement with vitality; Dr. Karl, who rejuvenated through nutrition; Mary, who rediscovered the value of sleep; Mickie, who reinvented herself at fifty-three and embraced life fully; and my father, who found purpose late in life. Each one's path is unique, just as yours will be.

No matter what has happened, know that you have gained wisdom from your journey. Thank your body for its patience and resilience. Let go of any regrets, for they are but stepping stones on your path. Treat yourself with the same kindness and self-love you would offer a dear friend. Trust in your body's innate wisdom and adaptability. Embrace the journey of discovering and redefining yourself.

As we raise a toast to the next ten years, let's celebrate the incredible, unstoppable force that is you! Remember, you're not merely aging; you're evolving into a vibrant sage—a person who embraces life's changes, harnesses the power of the five pillars, and lives with unwavering purpose, boundless energy, and timeless wisdom.

As you voyage toward vibrant aging, remember that every challenge is a doorway to opportunity, and every moment is a chance to become wiser, healthier, and more purposeful. May your life be brimming with vitality, ignited by passion, and enriched by the boundless joy of becoming the vibrant sage you were always meant to be. You hold the pen to your own story, and the chapters ahead are brimming with endless possibilities, waiting to be explored by the vibrant sage within you.

ACKNOWLEDGMENTS

First, I want to acknowledge you, dear reader; you were my inspiration. During periods when I felt overwhelmed and questioned myself, I would always come back to this little voice in my head that kept telling me I had to complete and publish this book. Even if I only change one life, it was worth sharing my journey and the pillars of vibrant aging. The world is abundant with vibrant sages, some of whom are already walking this path and others who are seeking guidance on aging with vibrancy and health. I hope this book has provided inspiration and guidance to live with enthusiasm and confidence. Embrace aging and the rest of your life! Thank you for being my motivation.

To all my speech pathology and fitness and health coaching clients. Thank you for trusting me in your health journey, sharing your challenges with me, and allowing me the opportunity to assist you in achieving your goals. I truly believe that in life, when we keep our hearts and minds open, we are both the teacher and the student within most of our relationships. This book would not have been possible without you.

Family

To my father, Henry T. Waring, whose courage and tenacity in the face of adversity continue to inspire me every day. Dad, your resilience and determination, which yielded three decades of life beyond all expectations, have shaped my outlook on life and fueled my passion for empowering others to live vibrantly. Your spirit lives on in every page of this book, and I dedicate it to you with all my love.

To my mother, Mary Ruth Jenkins, whose life was cut short at sixty-two. Oh, how much I have missed you . . . you should have had many more years. Yet you have been an inspiration as I struggle with doubts and uncertainty that this book may not be enough. But I realize I have done my job if this book helps just one other parent improve their health and vitality so they can give to their family and the world.

To my older siblings, Kay, Jim, and Betty, and my almost Irish twin, Nick, who have been my pillars of inspiration throughout my life. Each of you embodies the essence of a vibrant sage in your own unique way, showing me that age is just a number and that life is meant to be lived to the fullest. Thank you for being my lifelong models on this adventure called aging.

To my wonderful adult children, Allison, Stephen, and Sara, and my grandchildren, Amaury and Kristna. Having you in my life, the love you show—especially the grandchildren . . . love so pure. This book is my own personal reminder to take care of myself so I can be here for you.

Professional Support

To Kelli Watson, my first writing coach, whose unwavering belief in my story and guidance helped me find my voice as a writer. Kelli, you saw my potential from the beginning, and I'm grateful for your encouragement and wisdom as I embarked on this writing journey.

To the unnamed editor whose insightful feedback challenged me to rethink the premise of my book and ensure it resonated with my readers. Your constructive criticism pushed me to dig deeper and craft a story that truly inspires and empowers.

ACKNOWLEDGMENTS

To Jared Rosen, whose serendipitous connection brought clarity and purpose to my writing process. Jared, your guidance and support over the past two years have been invaluable, helping me refine my message and infuse my story with authenticity and relatability.

To Donna Schwontkowski, MS, DC, whose expertise as an editor and holistic health practitioner elevated the quality of my manuscript. Donna, your keen eye for detail and commitment to excellence inspired me to bring more creativity and storytelling into my writing.

To Joyce Walker, my final editor, whose belief in the importance of my message and dedication to my project helped me bring *The Vibrant Sage* to life. Joyce, your knowledge and guidance were instrumental in shaping the final version of this book, and I'm deeply grateful for your partnership.

Personal Support

Last but certainly not least, to my husband, Rob, whose unwavering support, guidance, and encouragement sustained me through the highs and lows of the writing process. Rob, your belief in me and the importance of my message never wavered, and I couldn't have completed this book without you by my side. Thank you for being my rock and assisting me in my journey as a vibrant sage.

RESOURCES

Even before beginning the process of writing this book, I was deeply interested in the subject of longevity. And the desire to learn more only intensified as I crafted these pages. Although their direct inclusion within these chapters may be absent, the wisdom gleaned from these works ignited within me a fervent thirst for understanding and a profound appreciation for the aging process, encouraging me to embrace it fully. Recognizing ourselves as conductors of our own bodies and lives, I owe a debt of gratitude to the following exceptional authors and their transformative books:

Attia, Peter, MD. *Outlive: The Science and Art of Longevity.* New York: Harmony Books, 2023.

Beasley, Elizabeth. "How Exercise Can Improve Your Sex Drive." *Healthgrades.* September 7, 2020. https://www.healthgrades.com/right-care/sexual-health/how-exercise-can-improve-your-sex-drive.

Blackburn, Elisabeth, PhD, and Elissa Epel, PhD. *The Telomere Effect.* New York: Grand Central Publishing, 2017.

Brager, Allison. *Meathead: Unraveling the Athletic Brain.* Bloomington, IN: Westbo Press, 2015.

Chan, Lillian So, and Manny W. Radomski, PhD. "Feel (and Look) Good from the Inside Out." *Ixcela.* https://ixcela.com/resources/feel-and-look-good-from-the-inside-out.html.

Cohut, Maria. "How Lack of Sleep Harms Circulation." *Medical News Today.* May 23, 2019. https://www.medicalnewstoday.com/articles/325267.

Dobkin, Carlie. "Science Says to Have More Sex for Better Sleep." *Eightsleep*. April 25, 2017. https://blog.eightsleep.com/sex-before-bed-is-worth-it/.

Fatouros, Ioannis G., Antonios Kambas, Ioannis Katrabasas, Diamanda Leontsini, Athanasios Chatzinikolaou, Athanasios Z. Jamurtas, Ioannis Douroudos, Nikolaos Aggelousis, and Kiriakos Taxildaris. "Resistance Training and Detraining Effects on Flexibility Performance in the Elderly Are Intensity-Dependent." *Journal of Strength and Conditioning Research* 20, no. 3 (2006): 634–42. https://pubmed.ncbi.nlm.nih.gov/16937978/.

Ferris, Emma. "9 Amazing Facts about Breathing." *Thebreatheffect*. December 26, 2018. https://www.thebreatheffect.com/facts-about-breathing.

"Finding Purpose in Life." *Harvard Health*. February 1, 2018. https://www.health.harvard.edu/staying-healthy/finding-purpose-in-life.

"Gasses: We Breathe In and Breathe Out." *Byjus*. September 4, 2018. https://byjus.com/biology/composition-gases-breathe/.

Gehrke, Sarah, MSN, RN. "ACLS Guide: Human Respiratory System—Parts and Functions." *Pacificmedicalacls*. Accessed December 14, 2021. https://pacificmedicalacls.com/acls-guide-to-the-human-respiratory-system.

Health Me Up. "Sex Drive Foods: Top 12 Foods to Improve Sex Drive." *Times of India*. November 5, 2014. https://timesofindia.indiatimes.com/life-style/health-fitness/diet/top-12-foods-to-improve-sex-drive/articleshow/21052188.cms.

Hensley, Laura. "5 Ways That Exercise Affects Your Sex Life." *Aaptiv*. June 2, 2018. https://aaptiv.com/magazine/exercise-affects-your-sex-life.

"Hormones." *MedlinePlus*. https://medlineplus.gov/hormones.html.

"Immune System." *Clevelandclinic*. Accessed December 14, 2021. https://my.clevelandclinic.org/health/articles/21196-immune-system.

Kaplin, Adam, and Laura Anzaldi. "New Movement in Neuroscience: A Purpose-Driven Life." *Cerebrum: The Dana Forum on Brain Science*. July 1, 2015. https://www.ncbi.nlm.nih.gov/pmc/articles/PMC4564234/.

Koizumi, Megumi., Hiroshi Ito, Yoshihiro Kaneko, and Yutaka Motohashi. "Effect of Having a Sense of Purpose in Life on the Risk of

Death from Cardiovascular Diseases." *J Epidemiology* 18, no. 5 (2008): 191–96. https://pubmed.ncbi.nlm.nih.gov/18753736/.

Li, Xiang, Qiaochu Xue, Mengying Wang, Tao Zhou, Hao Ma, Yoriko Heianza, and Lu Qi. "Adherence to a Healthy Sleep Pattern and Incident Heart Failure: A Prospective Study of 408,802 UK Biobank Participants." *Circulation*. November 16, 2020. https://doi.org/10.1161/CIRCULATIONAHA.120.050792.

Livni, Ephrat. "A Sense of Purpose Could Prolong Your Life." *Quartz*. May 25, 2019. https://qz.com/1628452/a-sense-of-purpose-could-prolong-your-life/.

Masters, Alina, Seithikurippu R. Pandi-Perumal, Azizi Seixas, Jean-Louis Girardin, and Samy I. McFarlane. "Melatonin, the Hormone of Darkness: From Sleep Promotion to Ebola Treatment." *Brain Disorders & Therapy* 4, no. 1 (January 2014). https://www.ncbi.nlm.nih.gov/pmc/articles/PMC4334454/.

Mintz, Laurie. "If You Want Better Sex, You Need Better Sleep." *Vice*. March 13, 2018. https://www.vice.com/en/article/3k734b/how-sleep-affects-sex-life.

Musich, Shirley, Shaohung S. Wang, Sandra Kraemer, Kevin Hawkins, and Ellen Wicker. "Purpose in Life and Positive Health Outcomes among Older Adults." *Population Health Management*. April 1, 2018. https://doi.org/10.1089/pop.2017.0063.

Paddock, Catharine, PhD. "Why Sleep Is Good for Your Arteries." *MedicalNewsToday*. February 21, 2019. https://www.medicalnewstoday.com/articles/324510.

Pelletier, Kenneth R., MD. *Change Your Genes, Change Your Life*. Carlsbad, CA: Hay House, 2018.

Philips. "Sleep Smart: Bolstering Immunity with Better Sleep." *Philips*. May 20, 2020. https://www.philips.com/a-w/about/news/archive/standard/news/articles/2020/20200520-sleep-smart-bolstering-immunity-with-better-sleep.html.

Prairie, Beth A., Michael F. Scheier, Karen A. Matthews, Chung-Chou H. Chang, and Rachel Hess. "A Higher Sense of Purpose in Life Is Associated with Sexual Enjoyment in Midlife Women." *Menopause (New York, NY)* 18, no. 8 (August 2011): 839–44. https://doi.org/10.1097/gme.0b013e31820befca.

Rediger, Jeffrey. *CURED: The Life-Changing Science of Spontaneous Healing.* New York: Flatiron Books, 2020.

Rodriguez, Julia. "Sufficient Sleep Improves Libido in Women." *Sleepdr.* April 4, 2015. https://www.sleepdr.com/the-sleep-blog/sufficient-sleep-improves-libido-in-women/.

Rodulfo, Kristina. "Sleep Deprivation Is the Same as Being Drunk, Study Says." *Elle.* April 5, 2016. https://www.elle.com/beauty/health-fitness/news/a35349/lack-of-sleep-same-as-being-drunk-uk-sleep-study/.

Roth, Erica, and Rena Goldman. "Top Foods to Enhance Your Sex Life." *Healthline.* July 17, 2020. https://www.healthline.com/health/7-foods-enhance-your-sex-life.

Sandoiu, Ana. "Does Having a Purpose in Life Help You Sleep Better?" *MedicalNewsToday.* July 15, 2017. https://www.medicalnewstoday.com/articles/318377.

Schaefer, Anna. "Better Sex: Workouts to Boost Your Performance," *Healthline.* October 10, 2019. https://www.healthline.com/health/better-sex-workouts-boost-performance?utm_medium=email&utm_source=email-share&utm_campaign=social-sharebar-referred-desktop.

Shumway, Allyse. "Aging Takes a Toll on Your Muscle Tissue. Researchers Discover One Type of Activity Puts This Process in Reverse." *healthtree.* April 15, 2020. https://healthtree.org/myeloma/community/articles/researchers-find-that-aerobic-exercise-can-reverse-aging-effects-

Siddiqui, G.M., MD. "Sleep Well—Stay Healthy." *Lifelinehealthcarebd.* Accessed December 14, 2021. http://www.lifelinehealthcarebd.org/Sleep-Well-Stay-Healthy.

Sinclair, David A., PhD, with Matthew D. LaPlante. *Lifespan, Why We Age and Why We Don't Have To.* New York: Atria Books, 2019.

"Sleep and Sleep Disorders Data and Statistics." *Centers for Disease Control and Prevention.* September 13, 2021. https://www.cdc.gov/sleep/data_statistics.html.

Wheeler, Mark. "Be Happy: Your Genes May Thank You for It." *UCLA Health.* July 29, 2013. https://newsroom.ucla.edu/releases/don-t-worry-be-happy-247644.

Williamson, Graham. "Maximum Phonation Time (MPT)." *Sltinfo.* February 1, 2014. https://www.sltinfo.com/maximum-phonation-time/.

CONNECT WITH THE EXPERTS

As promised, here is the contact and social media information for each of the experts I interviewed. Their profound insights, vast knowledge, and unwavering passion have been as inspiring to me as I hope they are to you. The richness of their personal journeys, coupled with the vulnerability they displayed while sharing their stories, adds depth and wisdom to further inspire each of us on our unique travels through aging and life.

Michaël Bijker, Breathwork Expert

- Website: www.yogalap.com
- Email: mailing@ews.yogalap.com
- Instagram: @life_awareness_project
- Facebook: Michael Bijker—Life Awareness Project
- YouTube: Michael Bijker—Life Awareness Project

Cathy Madeo, Fitness Expert

- Website: catymadeoyoga.com
- Instagram: @cathymadeoyoga
- Facebook: Cathy Madeo Yoga
- YouTube: Cathy Madeo Yoga
- Email: cathy@cathymadeoyoga.com

Karl Goldkamp, ND, Nutrition Expert

- Website: Keto Naturopath

- YouTube: Dr. Karl Goldkamp—Keto Naturopath
- Facebook: Karl Goldkamp
- Instagram: @karlgoldkamp
- Podcast: Dr. Karl Goldkamp—Keto Naturopath

Allison Brager, PhD, Sleep Expert

- Book: *Meathead: Unraveling the Athletic Brain,* published February 10, 2015.
- LinkedIn: Allison Brager
- Instagram: @docjockzzz
- Twitter: @docjockzzz

Mickie Zada, Living with Purpose Expert

- Facebook: Cool Retired Women Group
- LinkedIn: Mickie Zada
- Book: *Looking Behind Closed Doors: Domestic Abuse—If We Don't Change, Nothing Changes,* published July 2018.

Stephanie Bathurst, PhD, Sex Expert and Therapist

- Website: Bathurst Family Therapy
- Facebook: Bathurst Family Therapy
- Email: BathurstFamilyTherapy@gmail.com
- YouTube: @BathurstFamilyTherapy4766
- Instagram: @dr.StephanieBathurst

Don't forget me! I would love to hear from you. Let me know if I can assist you in your journey to becoming a Vibrant Sage!

To living life with energy and vitality (and a little spice),

Nancy

ABOUT THE AUTHOR

Nancy Waring is a seasoned professional with a passion for helping others unlock the boundless energy that lies within them. With a master's degree in speech pathology from Boston University and over three decades of experience in the field, coupled with a decade-long journey in health and fitness, her mission is to empower aging adults to reclaim their vitality and live the fulfilling lives they've always envisioned.

She holds many professional certifications, including NASM Certified Personal Trainer, Primal Health Coach, and RYT 500 Yoga Teacher, and is also a breath work facilitator, certified barre instructor, fitness nutrition specialist, and functional aging specialist.

Outside of her professional endeavors, Nancy finds fulfillment in family, friends, and her two dogs, Duke and Dimetri. With three grown children and two grandchildren, she cherishes family time. Residing in Boca Raton, Florida, Nancy enjoys traveling, yoga, being in nature, and cooking alongside her husband.

Made in the USA
Middletown, DE
04 December 2024